Writing Cornerstones

PARAGRAPHS IN CONTEXT

Leslie Dupont

University of Arizona

Longman

New York   San Francisco   Boston
London   Toronto   Sydney   Tokyo   Singapore   Madrid
Mexico City   Munich   Paris   Cape Town   Hong Kong   Montreal

Vice President and Publisher: Joseph Terry
Senior Acquisitions Editor: Steven Rigolosi
Senior Marketing Manager: Melanie Craig
Supplements Editor: Donna Campion
Media Supplements Editor: Nancy Garcia
Production Manager: Joseph Vella
Project Coordination, Photo Research, Text Design, and Electronic Page Makeup:
    Electronic Publishing Services Inc., N.Y.C.
Cover Designer/Manager: Nancy Danahy
Cover Illustration: Stone Wall © PhotoDisc, Inc. (retouched)
Manufacturing Buyer: Al Dorsey
Printer and Binder: R.R. Donnelley & Sons
Cover Printer: Coral Graphics Services

Photo Credit
page 35: ©Michael Nicholson/CORBIS

Library of Congress Cataloging-in-Publication Data

DuPont, Leslie.
    Writing cornerstones: paragraphs in context/Leslie Dupont.--1st ed.
     p. cm.
    Includes bibliographical references and index.
    ISBN 0-321-07865-9
     1. English language--Paragraphs--Problems, exercises, etc. 2. English
    language--Rhetoric--Problems, exercises, etc. 3. Report writing--Problems,
    exercises, etc. I. Title.

    PE1439 .D87 2002
    808'.042--dc21

                                                    2002019029

Please visit our website at http://www.ablongman.com/dupont

ISBN 0-321-07865-9

1 2 3 4 5 6 7 8 9 10—DOC—05 04 03 02

Dedication

This book and all others are dedicated to the many students I have worked with and look forward to working with for decades to come.
You are my teachers.

Brief Contents

Detailed Contents   *vii*

ESL Contents   *xiii*

Preface   *xv*

CHAPTER 1   Writing Backgrounds and Styles: Knowing Yourself   **1**

CHAPTER 2   What Makes an Effective Paragraph?   **15**

CHAPTER 3   Audience and Context: Your Reader(s) and Other Influences on Your Writing   **30**

CHAPTER 4   Reading and Writing *Are* Connected   **50**

CHAPTER 5   Invention: Strategies for Getting Started   **59**

CHAPTER 6   Making Meaning   **70**

CHAPTER 7   Revision and Content Development: Getting from the First Draft to the Final Draft   **81**

CHAPTER 8   Working on Your Paragraphs   **101**

CHAPTER 9   Proofreading: The Final Step   **111**

CHAPTER 10   Format: Professional Presentation   **170**

Appendix 1: Glossary   *181*

Appendix 2: Business and Technical Writing   *187*

Appendix 3: Modes of Discourse/Rhetorical Modes   *193*

More Resources about Writing   *197*

Index   *199*

Detailed Contents

ESL Contents   *xiii*

Preface   *xv*

CHAPTER 1   Writing Backgrounds and Styles: Knowing Yourself   1

PART 1: WHAT'S THE POINT?   1

Standard Written English: What Is It?   2
Language Challenges   2
What Is Oral Literacy?   5
   Storytelling   *5*
   Sermons and Hymns   *5*
   Community Gatherings   *6*
   Speeches   *6*
   Lectures   *6*
Learning To Be an Apprentice   7

PART 2: APPLICATIONS   8

1-1: Brainstorming Your Roots   8
1-2: Asking *How* and *Why*   12

CHAPTER 2   What Makes an Effective Paragraph?   15

PART 1: WHAT'S THE POINT?   15

The Writing Process   16
   Linear   *16*
   Circular   *16*
   Private-to-Public   *16*
Myths and Truths about Paragraphs   17

PART 2: APPLICATIONS   24

2-1: Working with Language and Content   24
2-2: Analyzing Paragraphs   26

CHAPTER 3   **Audience and Context:** Your Reader(s) and Other Influences on Your Writing   **30**

PART 1: WHAT'S THE POINT?   **30**

Audience: What Is It Really?   31
  Readers' Ages   31
  Readers' Backgrounds   31
  Readers' Expectations   31
Credibility   32
  Support   32
  Tone   32
Ways of Communicating   33
  Purpose   33
  Form   34
Context: What Is It?   34
  Time   34
  Place   36
  Language   36
  Internal Concerns   36

PART 2: APPLICATIONS   **38**

3-1: Paragraphs for Different Audiences   38
3-2: Identifying Audiences through Tone and Vocabulary   41
3-3: Identifying and Analyzing Audiences for Advertisements   41
3-4: Identifying and Analyzing Audiences for Coupons   42
3-5: Describe Yourself as an Audience   43
3-6: Rewriting a Paragraph   46
3-7: Different Languages for Different Writing Purposes   47
3-8: Analyzing an Advertisement   47
3-9: Analyzing a Magazine Cover   48

CHAPTER 4   **Reading and Writing *Are* Connected**   **50**

PART 1: WHAT'S THE POINT?   **50**

Why Do Reading and Writing Relate to One Another?   51
Understanding Clear Written Expression   51
Other Benefits of Reading   52

PART 2: APPLICATIONS   **53**

4-1: How Would You Write About ... ?   53

4-2: What Would You Want as a Reader From ... ?   54

4-3: Forms of Prose Style: How Does Reading a Certain Kind of Document
Help You Write a Certain Kind of Document?   56

CHAPTER 5   Invention: Strategies for Getting Started   **59**

PART 1: WHAT'S THE POINT?   59

Brainstorming   60
Learning Styles and Invention   60
Oral Brainstorming   60
   Taping   60
   Talking   60
   Reading Aloud   60
   Background Noise   60
Visual Brainstorming   60
   Drawing   60
   Note Cards   61
   Blocks   61
Kinesthetic (Movement-Based) Brainstorming   61
   Compose and Move   61
   Change Positions   61
Writing-Based Brainstorming   61
   Listing   61
   Clustering   61
   Freewriting   62
   Focused Freewriting   63
   Outlining   64
Invention during the Composing Process   65

PART 2: APPLICATIONS   66

5-1: Freewriting about an Advertisement   66
5-2: Focused Freewriting about an Advertisement   66
5-3: Creating a Cluster   67
5-4: Identifying a Focus from a Cluster   68
5-5: Creating an Outline   69

CHAPTER 6   Making Meaning   **70**

PART 1: WHAT'S THE POINT?   70

Words: Denotation vs. Connotation   71
Unity   71
   Topic Sentences   72
   Transitions   73

Organization   75
Outlining   75

PART 2: APPLICATIONS   76

6-1: Topic Sentences   76
6-2: Personal Chart of Transitional Words   77
6-3: Paragraph   78
6-4: Peer Review   78
6-5: Unifying Your Writing   79
6-6: Creating a New Paragraph   80

CHAPTER 7   Revision and Content Development: Getting from the First Draft to the Final Draft   81

PART 1: WHAT'S THE POINT?   81

Organization   82
Style   82
Revising a Paragraph   83
Other Ways to Revise   87
Content Development   87
Who Is/Are Your Reader(s)?   87
Thoroughness vs. Paragraph Length   89
Developing Ideas vs. Simply Repeating Them   90

PART 2: APPLICATIONS   92

7-1: Using Analogies   92
7-2: Paragraph   94
7-3: Supporting Examples   94
7-4: Paragraph with Examples   95
7-5: Style: Cleaning Up Your Sentences   95

CHAPTER 8   Working on Your Paragraphs   101

PART 1: WHAT'S THE POINT?   101

Portfolios: Gathering Your Best Work   102
Workshops   102
In the Classroom   102
Outside of the Classroom   102
One-on-One Peer Evaluation   103

PART 2: APPLICATIONS   105

8-1: Portfolio   105

8-2 Workshop Your Own Paragraph   106
8-3: Group-Workshopping Handout   106
8-4: One-on-One Peer-Evaluation Handout   107
8-5: Group-Workshopping Styles/Activities   108
8-6: One-on-One Peer Evaluation   110

CHAPTER 9   **Proofreading:** The Final Step   **111**

PART 1: WHAT'S THE POINT?   **111**

Punctuation   112
Period   113
Comma   114
    Addresses   115
    Dates   115
Semicolon   115
Colon   117
Apostrophe   117
Question Mark   118
Quotation Marks   118
Parentheses   119
Hyphen   119
Dash   120
Exclamation Mark   121
Typos and Omissions   121
Other Grammatical Issues   121
    Singular and Plural Forms   121
    Subject-Verb Agreement   123
    Pronunciation   123
    Idioms/Idiomatic Expressions   124
    Prepositions   124
    Definite and Indefinite Articles   125
Spelling   127
    S on Word Endings   127
    "I before E"   127
    Single and Double Consonants   127
    Commonly Misspelled Words (Common Homonyms)   127
    Using Spell-Check   128

PART 2: APPLICATIONS   **129**

9-1: Proofreading Questions to Ask Yourself   129
9-2: Punctuation 1   129
9-3: Punctuation 2   152
9-4: Proofreading Paragraphs   155

9-5: Proofreading Your Own Paragraphs   168
9-6: Small-Group Proofreading   169

CHAPTER 10   **Format:** Professional Presentation   **170**

PART 1: WHAT'S THE POINT?   **170**

How Your Presentation Affects Your Readers   171
> *Consistency and Audience Expectations   171*

Formatting Basics   171
> *Margins   171*
> *Alignment   171*
> *Justification   171*
> *Titles   172*
> *Paragraph Indentation   172*
> *Headings and Subheadings   172*
> *Headers and Footers   173*
> *White (or Negative) Space   173*
> *Twelve-Point Font Size   173*

Common Documentation Styles: MLA and APA   173
> *MLA   173*
> *APA   174*

PART 2: APPLICATIONS   **176**

10-1: Designing a Paragraph Layout   176
10-2: Small-Group Discussion of Formatting   176
10-3: Documentation-Style Setup   177
10-4: Using Subheadings   178
10-5: Text Justification   179

Appendix 1: Glossary   *181*

Appendix 2: Business and Technical Writing   *187*

Appendix 3: Modes of Discourse/Rhetorical Modes   *193*

More Resources about Writing   *197*

Index   *199*

ESL Contents

This table of contents is more focused on the needs of English-as-second-language students. Don't worry if you can't find matching headings. Many of the entries in this table of contents point you to specific sections and page numbers.

Chapter 1   Writing Backgrounds and Styles: Knowing Yourself   1
Standard Written English: What Is It?   2
Language Challenges   2
Pronunciation   4

Chapter 4   Reading and Writing *Are* Connected   50
Clear Written Expression   51
Prose Styles   56

Chapter 5   Invention: Strategies for Getting Started   59
Brainstorming   60
  Oral Brainstorming   60
  Visual Brainstorming   60
  Kinesthetic (Movement-Based) Brainstorming   61
  Writing-Based Brainstorming   61
    Listing   61
    Clustering   61
    Freewriting   62
    Focused Freewriting   63
    Outlining   64

Chapter 6   Making Meaning   70
Denotation vs. Connotation   71
Topic Sentences   72
Transitions   73

Chapter 7   Revision and Content Development: Getting from the First Draft
to the Final Draft   81
Wordiness   82

Sentence Structure   84
Word Choice   86
Other Ways to Revise   87
Content Development   87
Who Are Your Readers?   87
Analogies   91

Chapter 8   Working on Your Paragraphs   101
Portfolios   102
Workshops   102
One-on-One Peer Evaluation   103

Chapter 9   Proofreading: The Final Step   111
Punctuation   112

Period   113
Comma   114
Semicolon   115
Colon   117
Apostrophe   117
Question Mark   118
Quotation Marks   118
Parentheses   119
Hyphen   119
Dash   120
Exclamation Mark   121

Singular and Plural Forms   121

Verbs   121
Nouns   122
Adjectives   122

Subject-Verb Agreement   123
Pronunciation   123
Idioms/Idiomatic Expressions   124
Prepositions   124
Definite and Indefinite Articles   125
Spelling   127

Homonyms   127

Chapter 10   Format: Professional Presentation   170
Formatting   171
Common Documentation Styles: MLA and APA   173

Appendix 1: Glossary   *181*

Preface

As writers and human beings, each of us requires more than a sentence, paragraph, or essay "blueprint" to engage with writing—at any level. Writing must be meaningful and audience aware; to remain engaged, the audience immediately must be able to connect with what they are reading. What is important is *doing* the act of writing as you explore various aspects of writing.

Writers come from a variety of writing and speaking backgrounds, and any book on writing, to be effective, must address these backgrounds. Today's typical community college student population, for instance, contains many ESL and limited English proficiency (LEP) students. In addition, many college students are now familiar with visual media like television and computer and video games. These and other students are more used to seeing and talking than reading and writing. In addition, students come from a variety of cultural backgrounds in which writing takes varying levels of importance, from essential to nonexistent. Finally, many students have attention deficit disorder (ADD) or learning disabilities (such as dyslexia). This variety of backgrounds and learning styles demands a flexible approach to writing that understands how wonderfully "messy" the writing process is. A primary goal of this book is to honor multiple writer backgrounds and learning styles.

GOALS AND THEMES

This book's primary goal is to approach writing by honoring writers' widely varied backgrounds and learning styles. *Writing Cornerstones* incorporates student writing experiences and the various writing contexts encountered in college—aiming to help students gain flexibility in writing situations.

A second goal is to help students surmount fear-based and other barriers to writing, encouraging them to approach college writing with increased comfort and confidence. To encourage this a large part of each chapter is comprised of real-world and academic writing applications from which students and teachers can draw.

CONTENT OVERVIEW

Chapter One, "Writing Backgrounds and Styles: Knowing Yourself," introduces students to themselves as writers by having them explore their own backgrounds to become conscious of their individual writing patterns and the influences on their attitudes toward writing.

Chapter Two, "What Makes an Effective Paragraph?" breaks through myths about paragraphs and immediately models paragraphs that work well and explains why they do. In this chapter, students are encouraged not only to begin writing paragraphs but also to begin thinking critically about what makes a paragraph effective or ineffective.

Chapter Three, "Audience and Context: Your Reader(s) and Other Influences on Your Writing," establishes the importance of knowing why you are writing and whom you're writing to. Readers establish the tone, purpose, and content of any piece of public writing, and knowing who they are allows a writer to make appropriate choices in these areas. In addition, this chapter introduces writers to the other surrounding influences on them and their writing: culture, value systems, time, place, and language.

Chapter Four, "Reading and Writing *Are* Connected," discusses the important idea that reading and writing influence each other heavily and cannot be separated.

Chapter Five, "Invention: Strategies for Getting Started," gets writers working with a wide variety of prewriting strategies that address many learning styles: writer-based, kinesthetic (movement-based), oral, visual, and aural.

Chapter Six, "Making Meaning," introduces writers to concepts of unity and organization in the paragraph. It provides activities that immediately apply structure to ideas.

Chapter Seven, "Revision and Content Development: Getting from the First Draft to the Final Draft," distinguishes between length and thoroughness, helping writers learn how to expand on ideas rather than simply repeat them. It establishes the importance of meaningful content at a paragraph level. It also presents revision as a lively, thoughtful process that is separate from proofreading.

Chapter Eight, "Working on Your Paragraphs," provides information and activities for working in and out of the classroom to improve your writing: showing each writer how others write, helping writers form writing and workshopping groups, and suggesting activities writers can do with their own and their peers' writing.

Chapter Nine, "Proofreading: The Final Step," sets out the basics of grammar and punctuation so that writers can improve their writing at the sentence level after revising content and organization. This chapter encourages writers to make connections between the mechanics of writing and the meaning behind these mechanics.

Chapter Ten, "Format: Professional Presentation," introduces writers to basic MLA and APA formatting and documentation styles.

CHAPTER ORGANIZATION

All chapters are divided into two major sections: "What's the Point?" and "Applications." The chapters and the activities within them may be used in any order desired by both students and instructors.

The down-to-earth nature of the question "What's the Point?" is designed to parallel the very valid questions that students have about writing and its usefulness. "Applications" sections not only help writers immediately apply what has been discussed in the preceding pages but also prepares them to write in a variety of contexts in and out of an academic setting.

UNIQUE FEATURES OF *WRITING CORNERSTONES*

- An ESL Table of Contents

- Writing activities for multiple learning styles

- Spaces within the text for writing, which allow writers to use this text as a workbook

- Incorporation of outside writing resources, both print and web based

- An appendix on technical writing basics

- Self-reflection activities to help writers identify their strengths for writing

- Separate chapters and emphases on revision, proofreading, and formatting

- Introduction to the basics of MLA and APA formats to familiarize writers with these two common documentation styles

- Writing activities that help writers to apply grammar basics in their own writing immediately

SUPPLEMENTS

The Teaching and Learning Package

A complete **instructor's manual** to accompany *Writing Cornerstones: Paragraphs in Context* is available (ISBN 0–321–07867–5). Prepared by the author, it features chapter descriptions and sample answers to applications, as well as sample syllabi, handouts, and lesson plans. These documents offer both new and experienced instructors clear plans for applying the textbook in the classroom. They also provide ready-to-use materials for instructors with limited preparation time.

A separate **test bank** is available, featuring quizzes for each chapter in the textbook. Ask your Longman sales rep for ISBN 0-321-07868-3.

Be sure to visit *Writing Cornerstones* online at http://www.ablongman.com/dupont. The web site features areas accessible to and aimed at two different audiences: instructors and students. It offers an overview of the textbook's layout and content; a .pdf version of the instructor's manual; and printable versions of handouts, lesson plans, and sample syllabi. In addition, it offers links for both instructors and students to relevant web sites for each chapter, a continuously expanding bibliography of relevant books and articles, a section on teaching tips, a glossary, and writing activities/exercises and reviews.

For Additional Reading and Reference

The Dictionary Deal Two dictionaries can be shrinkwrapped with *Writing Cornerstones* at a nominal fee. *The New American Webster Handy College Dictionary* is a paperback reference text with more than 100,000 entries. *Merriam Webster's Collegiate Dictionary*, tenth edition, is a hardback reference with a citation file of more than 14.5 million examples of English words drawn from actual use. For more information on how to shrinkwrap a dictionary with your text, please contact your Longman sales representative.

Penguin Quality Paperback Titles A series of Penguin paperbacks is available at a significant discount when shrinkwrapped with this text. Some titles available are Toni Morrison's *Beloved*, Julia Alvarez's *How the Garcia Girls Lost Their Accents*, Mark Twain's *Huckleberry Finn*, *Narrative of the Life of Frederick Douglass*, Harriet Beecher Stowe's *Uncle Tom's Cabin*, Dr. Martin Luther King, Jr.'s *Why We Can't Wait*, and plays by Shakespeare, Miller, and Albee. For a complete list of titles or more information, please contact your Longman sales consultant.

100 Things to Write About This 100-page book contains 100 individual assignments for writing on a variety of topics and in a wide range of formats, from expressive to analytical. Ask your Longman sales representative for a sample copy. 0-673-98239-4

***Newsweek* Alliance** Instructors may choose to shrinkwrap a 12-week subscription to *Newsweek* with any Longman text. The price of the subscription is 57 cents per issue (a total of $6.84 for the subscription). Available with the subscription is a free "Interactive Guide to *Newsweek*"—a workbook for students who are using the text. In addition, *Newsweek* provides a wide variety of instructor supplements free to teachers, including maps, Skill Builders, and weekly quizzes. For more information on the *Newsweek* program, please contact your Longman sales representative.

Electronic and Online Offerings

[NEW] The Longman Writer's Warehouse This innovative and exciting online supplement is the perfect accompaniment to any developmental writing course. Created by developmental English instructors specially for developing writers, The Writer's Warehouse covers every part of the writing process. Also included are journaling capabilities, multimedia activities, diagnostic tests, an interactive handbook, and a complete instructor's manual. The Writer's Warehouse requires no space on your school's server; rather, students complete and store their work on the Longman server, and are able to access it, revise it, and continue working at any time. For more details about how to shrinkwrap a free subscription to The Writer's Warehouse with this text, please contact your Longman sales representative. For a free guided tour of the site, visit http://longmanwriterswarehouse.com.

The Writer's ToolKit Plus   This CD-ROM offers a wealth of tutorial, exercise, and reference material for writers. It is compatible with either a PC or Macintosh platform and is flexible enough to be used either occasionally for practice or regularly in class lab sessions. For information on how to bundle this CD-ROM FREE with your text, please contact your Longman sales representative.

The Longman English Pages Web Site   Both students and instructors can visit our free content-rich Web site for additional reading selections and writing exercises. From the Longman English pages, visitors can conduct a simulated Web search, learn how to write a resume and cover letter, or try their hand at poetry writing. Stop by and visit us at http://www.ablongman.com/englishpages.

The Longman Electronic Newsletter   Twice a month during the spring and fall, instructors who have subscribed receive a free copy of the Longman Developmental English Newsletter in their e-mailbox. Written by experienced classroom instructors, the newsletter offers teaching tips, classroom activities, book reviews, and more. To subscribe, visit the Longman Developmental English Website at http://www.ablongman.com/basicskills, or send an e-mail to Basic Skills@ablongman.com.

For Instructors

[NEW] Electronic Test Bank for Writing   This electronic test bank features more than 5,000 questions in all areas of writing, from grammar to paragraphing, through essay writing, research, and documentation. With this easy-to-use CD-ROM, instructors simply choose questions from the electronic test bank, then print out the completed test for distribution. CD-ROM: 0-321-08117-X Print version: 0-321-08486-1

Competency Profile Test Bank, Second Edition   This series of 60 objective tests covers ten general areas of English competency, including fragments; comma splices and run-ons; pronouns; commas, and capitalization. Each test is available in remedial, standard, and advanced versions. Available as reproducible sheets or in computerized versions. Free to instructors. Paper version: 0-321-02224-6. Computerized IBM: 0-321-02633-0. Computerized Mac: 0-321-02632-2.

Diagnostic and Editing Tests and Exercises, Fifth Edition   This collection of diagnostic tests helps instructors access students' competence in Standard Written English for the purpose of placement or to gauge progress. Available as reproducible sheets or in computerized versions, and free to instructors. Paper: 0-321-11730-1. CD-ROM: 0-321-11732-8.

ESL Worksheets, Third Edition   These reproducible worksheets provide ESL students with extra practice in areas they find the most troublesome. A diagnostic test and post-test are provided, along with answer keys and suggested topics for writing. Free to adopters. 0-321-07765-2

Longman Editing Exercises   Fifty-four pages of paragraph editing exercises give students extra practice using grammar skills in the context of longer passages. Free when packaged with any Longman title. 0-205-31792-8.

80 Practices   A collection of reproducible, ten-item exercises that provide additional practices for specific grammatical usage problems, such as comma splices, capitalization, and pronouns. Includes an answer key, and free to adopters. 0-673-53422-7

CLAST Test Package, Fourth Edition   These two 40-item objective tests evaluate students' readiness for the CLAST exams. Strategies for teaching CLAST preparedness are included. Free with any Longman English title. Reproducible sheets: 0-321-01950-4 Computerized IBM version: 0-321-01982-2 Computerized Mac version: 0-321-01983-0

TASP Test Package, Third Edition   These 12 practice pre-tests and post-tests assess the same reading and writing skills covered in the TASP examination. Free with any Longman English title. Reproducible sheets: 0-321-01959-8 Computerized IBM version: 0-321-01985-7 Computerized Mac version: 0-321-01984-9

***Teaching Online: Internet Research, Conversation, and Composition*, Second Edition**   Ideal for instructors who have never surfed the Net, this easy-to-follow guide offers basic definitions, numerous examples, and step-by-step information about finding and using Internet sources. Free to adopters. 0-321-01957-1

Teaching Writing to the Non-Native Speaker   This booklet examines the issues that arise when non-native speakers enter the developmental classroom. Free to instructors, it includes profiles of international and permanent ESL students, factors influencing second-language acquisition, and tips on managing a multicultural classroom. 0-673-97452-9

For Students

[NEW] *The Longman Writer's Journal*   This journal for writers, free with *Writing Cornerstones*, offers students a place to think, write, and react. For an examination copy, contact your Longman sales consultant. 0-321-08639-2

[NEW] *The Longman Researcher's Journal*   This journal for writers and researchers, free with this text, helps students plan, schedule, write, and revise their research project. An all-in-one resource for first-time researchers, the journal guides students gently through the research process. 0-321-09530-8.

Researching Online, Sixth Edition   A perfect companion for a new age, this indispensable new supplement helps students navigate the Internet. Adapted from *Teaching Online*, the instructor's Internet guide, *Researching Online* speaks directly to students, giving them detailed, step-by-step instructions for performing electronic searches. Available free when shrinkwrapped with this text. 0-321-11733-6

Learning Together: An Introduction to Collaborative Theory   This brief guide to the fundamentals of collaborative learning teaches students how to work effectively in groups, how to revise with peer response, and how to co-author a paper or report. Shrinkwrapped free with any Longman Basic Skills text. 0-673-46848-8

A Guide for Peer Response, **Second Edition**   This guide offers students forms for peer critiques, including general guidelines and specific forms for different stages in the writing process. Also appropriate for freshman-level courses. Free to adopters. 0-321-01948-2

Thinking Through the Test, **by D.J. Henry**   This special workbook, prepared specially for students in Florida, offers ample skill and practice exercises to help students prep for the Florida State Exit Exam. To shrinkwrap this workbook free with your textbook, please contact your Longman sales representative. Available in two versions: with and without answers. Also available: Two laminated grids (one for reading, one for writing) that can serve as handy references for students preparing for the Florida State Exit Exam.

ACKNOWLEDGMENTS

I wish to thank the following people for their contributions to this book:
Louise Rodríguez Connal, Donella Eberle, Nancy Edmonds, Chris Hamel, Devon Holmes, Katharine Murphy-Jenness, Carol Nowotny-Young, Kate Oubre, Sharon Sandgathe, Maria-Elena Wakamatsu, and Elsa Wilson have provided insightful suggestions and moral support to me throughout this project. You are the powerful women in my world.

The many students I have worked with over the years—and the essential feedback they have given me about their writing processes.

Of course, I wish to thank my editor, Steven Rigolosi, who also worked with me to develop my ideas. Without his patience and encouragement, my ideas would have remained on the drawing board.

I would also like to thank the following reviewers for their insights into the manuscript:

Annie Lou Burns, Meridian Community College

Peg Ehlen, Ivy Technical State College

Laurie Esler, Southern Wesleyan University

Devon Holmes, University of Arizona

Dawn Leonard, Charleston Southern University

Leslie Dupont

CHAPTER 1

Writing Backgrounds and Styles
Knowing Yourself

Writing is a healing and creative journey back to the
mystery and power of our words as an instrument of
creation that came latent within us at birth.
—*G. Lynn Nelson*

PART 1: WHAT'S THE POINT?

By the time we get to college, most of us in the United
States are aware of the diverse culture in which we live.
Our different backgrounds incorporate various literacy
styles (ways in which we read, write, and speak). And our
individual minds have individual learning styles (how we
learn and how we figure things out). Finally, most of us do
not use **Standard English** in speaking or writing. In fact,
many of us don't even know what Standard English is or
why it's important. Below are various models of literacy and
learning, including Standard English. You will see yourself
in at least one of these models, and many of you will spot
yourselves in several.

STANDARD WRITTEN ENGLISH: WHAT IS IT?

Standard Written English is formal English, following specific and formal rules of **grammar** and expression. Have you ever heard of Castilian Spanish? Those of you who speak Spanish may know that this form of the language is far more formal than the Spanish you use to speak and write in everyday life. This is the same for Standard English, which schools frequently ask you to use. In addition, magazines like *Atlantic Monthly* and the *New Yorker* use Standard Written English, as do newspapers like the *Wall Street Journal* and the *New York Times*. College textbooks and many general nonfiction books also use Standard Written English. In our culture, knowing how and when to use Standard English is a mark of education and of ease and flexibility with forms of writing and speech.

Briefly, when colleges (for example, community colleges, universities, and business colleges) became more popular during the early and middle parts of the twentieth century, they began to set standards of excellence in writing, math, and the sciences. Standards were seen as a way to equalize and evaluate student abilities.

Positive Consequences of Using Standard English (SE)	Negative Consequences of Not Using Standard English (SE)
Language flexibility. More success in formal academic, career, and social situations. Greater understanding of written texts. Greater sophistication in language use. Higher salaries.	A need to catch up with written and spoken SE if you are not used to using it. Lower salaries. Limited understanding of written texts—and lots of discomfort with reading. Discomfort in formal academic, career, and social settings.

LANGUAGE CHALLENGES

Any of us attempting to learn a new language, especially as adults, frequently has to maintain a sense of humor and perspective. That isn't always easy to do as we struggle with limited vocabulary and stumble over rules of grammar. We can be highly literate in one (or more) language yet may be struggling with preschool literacy in another. Even when we get better at using a new language, we may still make errors because we are thinking in a different language or haven't used the new language long enough to work out certain grammatical details.

How many of you, for instance, speak a language in which there are no **definite** or **indefinite articles** (*the, a, an*)? Do you find yourselves leaving these tiny words out even though you know they are needed in English? Or do you find yourselves inserting them in the wrong places? What about those of you whose first language uses *s* on plural-verb or plural-adjective forms? Is it frustrating to you that English does just the opposite?

In the box below is an example of a language challenge I experienced as a teacher. It illustrates why a sense of humor is as important as practice in learning a new language or improving in your native language.

> One of the communities in which I teach is heavily Spanish speaking. For several years now, I have been listening to and learning as much Spanish as possible in order to communicate more effectively with some of the people I work with. However, I often make mistakes—sometimes quite amusing ones. One day, for instance, I answered the phone at the front desk, and the woman on the other end spoke to me in Spanish. I understood enough to figure out that she was the mother of one of my students and wanted to speak to me. I wanted to tell her that I was her daughter's teacher, but what came out was "Yo es si madre," which doesn't really translate into much of anything. (I sort of said, "I is she mother.") What I meant to say was, "Yo soy su maestra" ("I am her teacher"). Well, quite understandably, this earned a lot of laughs. I was a little embarrassed, but mostly I was amused because by now I was getting used to stumbling over myself in Spanish. It IS funny when we struggle with a new language—no doubt about it. It's *also* extremely important that we remember this struggle is *normal*. Sometimes, not only do we forget this but others do, too. Fortunately, I've developed a pretty thick skin about the messiness of this process, which has helped me relax and keep learning.

What people often forget is that these errors are normal because not only are they moving between languages, they are also moving between actual learning styles. If English is your first language, you might be challenged by not having done much reading or writing in a while. Or you might have attention deficit disorder (ADD) or a learning disability (LD). The problem can be that in college your written and spoken work is graded—often before you have gotten comfortable with college-level reading and writing.

Challenges

1. The Standard English context of most colleges provides little to no room for other literacy styles.
2. Many English-as-second-language (ESL) learners can feel stupid because they are awkward with writing, become

embarrassed at their grades and/or performance, and sometimes begin to avoid writing.

3. Many people who are comfortable speaking English are at
first unsure about how to read and/or write English.

Those of you whose first, or only, language is English also struggle with
written English at times. Preposition usage and subject-verb agreement (how
to identify plural or singular subjects and their correct verb forms) can be quite
challenging for all English speakers and writers.

Another major challenge is homonym usage. Don't let that term scare you!
Homonyms are simply words that sound the same but are spelled differently
and have different meanings (such as "there," "their," and "they're"). Using
computer spell-check programs can be challenging, too, because these programs don't let you know when you have used a wrong word that is spelled
right (like using "form" where you want to write "from").

In chapter 9, on proofreading, you will learn about doing a line-by-line
review of your writing so you don't depend only on spell-check (or grammar-
check) programs to help you. There is also a section on common homonyms
for your reference.

Those of you who are ESL students, then, need to develop a network of
people who understand your struggles and will work with you to develop flu-
ency (tutors and writing centers, for instance). Those of you who are just
rusty in reading and writing English also need a support network of people
to give you feedback while you practice. And those of you with ADD or an
LD need people and resources that can help you find reading and writing
techniques that work for you (e.g., composing in your mind while walking
on a treadmill, or reading sentences aloud). You also, however, need patience,
determination, and a good sense of humor, because learning *anything* is both
messy and funny.

Pronunciation

Pronunciation (how a word sounds) is a challenge for many
writers, some of whom are guessing at a word's spelling based on
how they think it would sound in their own language. For instance,
the Spanish *i* often sounds like the English *e*, and this can get quite
confusing to Spanish → English writers. A word often confused is
"this" (singular) for "these" (plural). This is simply due to pronunciation differences; however, it also demonstrates how reading and
writing can work together. If you know from reading that "this" is
a singular form, you will be less likely to confuse it with "these,"
even though your first language might suggest otherwise.

WHAT IS ORAL LITERACY?

Oral literacy simply means using speech to communicate—definitely more than and sometimes in place of writing.

Types of Oral Literacy

Story telling	Community gatherings	Sermons
Hymns	Speeches	Lectures

Storytelling   We teach each other about ourselves, our history and heritage, appropriate social behaviors, and our spirituality through the stories we tell each other. If you come from a background that uses many spoken stories to communicate ideas, beliefs, and values, then you have a wonderful resource at your disposal. To tell stories effectively, you need many details, vivid images, clear explanations, an inviting tone, and a strong sense of **audience**. All of these are components of effective writing, too.

Storytelling offers a helpful model for students who need to hear ideas spoken before writing them down. If speaking works better than writing for you, speak your ideas into a tape recorder or tell them to someone else first. Later, you can write them down and smooth them out.

Sermons and Hymns   You may have a lot of experience with sermons and hymns, particularly if you attend a Bible-based church. Sermons are intended to teach us about the god(s) and holy words/laws of our religions. Hymns are a form of religious/spiritual song that praises whom and what we believe in.

Sermons are commonly used in Bible-based religions (e.g., Pentecostal, Catholic, Baptist). To be effective, however, sermons must use details and examples that the listeners can apply to their own lives and experiences. Sermons must take the teachings of the church and present them in ways that listeners clearly understand; otherwise, listeners will not know how to apply these teachings in their lives. For instance, many preachers and priests use the parable of the prodigal son to teach forgiveness. Different styles work for different people, so the listeners are very important in deciding how formal or informal, emotional or objective the person giving the sermon wants to sound.

Hymns are meant to be sung as part of many religious ceremonies. Sometimes they are lively and loud; at other times they are formal and quiet. Again, it depends on the church and its members. In some situations churchgoers stand formally and quietly at their pews as they sing. In other church settings, people sway, clap, and dance to the music.

This same awareness of **tone** and **style** is essential in writing in order to make sure you are connecting with your readers. If hymns and sermons are part of your background, then you are already aware that what works well for some audiences may not work well for others.

Community Gatherings   Community gatherings can take many forms: town council meetings, powwows, informal discussions in the town square, lodge meetings, and so forth. If you want people to listen to you at a large gathering, then you have to figure out what is important to them and how you will gain their interest. At a powwow, which is a gathering of people from many American Indian nations, only dances that are appropriate for outsiders to see will be performed. Private ceremonial dances are only appropriate for the men or women within a specific tribal or spiritual community. Town council meetings are also for the public—members of a specific neighborhood, town, or city. People attend these meetings to hear the mayor and his or her council members decide on policies that will affect that community. They also come to speak out in favor of or against these policies. Some discussions about policies, however, will be held in private among the mayor and certain council members.

The **audience awareness** that you need to have in community gatherings can be extremely helpful to you when you are writing—especially when you are writing persuasive essays. Again, you will already have a sense of what works for some people and not for others.

Speeches   Speeches are usually **persuasive**—political campaign speeches, for instance. This means that the speaker is trying to get the audience to agree with him or her and take some sort of action (such as voting for or against an issue). If you have experience listening to and/or giving speeches, then you are already experienced in learning how to "read" your audiences and communicate effectively to them. And you also might know what it's like to misread your audience and give them an impression that you don't want to give them. For instance, speakers probably will not be listened to if they talk about closing a mine to the miners who work there, or if they are promoting deforestation to environmentalists.

Lectures   Lectures are a form of giving information to others by standing before them and speaking. As college students, you will probably attend both effective (interesting) and ineffective (boring) lectures at some point in your college careers. Learn from both the good and the bad lectures. They will show you how and how not to inform others about various subjects. If you simply drone on in your writing like a tired bumblebee, you might put your readers to sleep. If, however, you vary your tone, ask the readers questions, create manageable sections of writing, and then give your readers' eyes a break, you will keep your readers' attention.

LEARNING TO BE AN APPRENTICE

When we're not used to an idea, experience, or language, we can feel fear—fear of the unknown or unfamiliar. Fear of stumbling with language use in front of others. What we need to do is shift our perspectives toward being apprentices. An apprentice is just beginning to learn a craft or a trade (in this case, writing, reading, and/or speaking Standard English). It is natural, then, for apprentices to have many questions about their subjects. It is also natural for them to stumble, make mistakes, do a lot of practicing, and work with mentors/teachers who can help them understand and use new techniques, styles, and words.

Apprenticeship is very much a part of learning. For instance, when you bring a strong oral-literacy background to college, you immediately become an apprentice because suddenly you are in a strong written-literacy environment. However, even if you have a lot of reading and writing experience, when faced with more advanced reading and writing, you are *also* an apprentice. This is also true for ESL students, students with **limited English proficiency (LEP)**, and students with attention deficit disorder or learning disabilities (e.g., dyslexia). In fact, each of us is an apprentice at some point or another—usually more than once in our lifetimes.

Thinking of yourself as an apprentice helps you stay open to new ideas and to taking risks with your writing. It allows you to experiment and make mistakes because you no longer are pressuring yourself to be an expert or to write perfectly.

So, how do you shift your perspective to that of an apprentice?

Well, you will have to do lots of reading and writing. In addition, you will do lots of thinking and talking about what you've read and written, finding new ways to use words, practicing rules of grammar and punctuation, experimenting with different styles, and so forth. However, you don't need to do all of this in a single day; you do it step by step. Here is where patience and determination are big helps.

PART 2: APPLICATIONS

In this section, you will explore your own writing/reading/speaking history—some of the influences that have caused you to have the perspectives (positive, negative, or both) you have about writing, reading, and speaking. Working through and discussing the following activities will give you more clarity about who you think you are as a writer and reader. It is amazing how much can influence each of us in these areas.

APPLICATION 1-1: Brainstorming Your Roots

When you dig around in your roots, your beginnings, you can become much clearer about why and how you have grown the way you have. Who are you now? What beliefs, fears, and enjoyment about writing (and reading) do you bring with you when you enter a classroom or begin a course—or simply sit down to a blank piece of paper or computer screen? Let's begin exploring all of this with some brainstorming. To brainstorm is to come up with ideas that you can write about.

Complete the following phrases with lists of statements that describe you. Once you have completed one or more lists, just write freely, using what you have listed. If you want to attempt a paragraph, go ahead, but you do not have to yet. The point is to practice putting your ideas on paper. You can also speak them into a tape recorder, draw pictures, talk while on a stationary bicycle, or do whatever else works to get your ideas out. The notebook spaces below are there to help some of you get started. Use them only if you find them helpful—some of you will, and some of you won't.

I live:

_____

_____

_____

_____

_____

_____

_____

_____

_____

I come from:

_____

_____

_____

_____

_____

_____

_____

I am afraid of:

_____

_____

_____

_____

_____

_____

_____

I like:

_____

_____

_____

_____

_____

_____

_____

_____

I am good at:

_____

_____

_____

_____

_____

_____

_____

_____

I don't like:

_____

_____

_____

_____

_____

_____

_____

_____

_____

_____

List any words and phrases that come to mind when you think of the following four activities:

Writing
Reading
Thinking
Speaking

Weaknesses I think I have in writing, reading, and/or thinking	Weaknesses others have convinced me I have in writing, reading, and/or thinking	Strengths I think I have in writing, reading, and/or thinking	Strengths others have convinced me I have in writing, reading, and/or thinking

APPLICATION 1-2: Asking *How* and *Why*

When you ask how and why, you are exploring what an idea, issue, text, experience, or image means. You want to learn what it stands for, how it affects you, who created it and why, what it teaches you and/or others, what its point is, or how it relates (or doesn't relate) to your world. Asking how and why gives you deeper understanding and insight into yourself and into what surrounds you.

Review the writing you did for the previous application. Ask yourself *why* you came up with the answers you did. For now, just begin answering this question. You don't need to organize your answers yet; just get the ideas down on paper. You can begin here, but you'll probably need to move on to notebook paper or a journal at some point.

➤   Before you begin, here is an example:

> "I wrote that I live a busy life because I am always doing something. But I like it this way; otherwise, I get bored. Why do I get bored? I guess because my mind races and my body gets restless, thinking about lots of things at once, and if I don't keep them occupied, restless thoughts and energy build up...."

This is not meant to be a great piece of writing, but it is getting some ideas out that the writer can work with later during revision.

_____

_____

_____

_____

_____

_____

_____

_____

_____

As you begin asking and answering these questions, you will probably have to stop from time to time. You might run out of ideas quickly at first; this is normal. Just chip away at it and the ideas will come. I have scattered various examples around the next couple of pages so you can see what you are being asked to do.

At seven, I remember my mother yelling at me to "put that silly book down" and help her with the housework....

Now ask yourself *how* you came to have the above characteristics. Begin answering this question here if you would like, but feel free to move on to notebook paper or a journal whenever you feel comfortable doing so.

When I was growing up, I was either inside reading or outside climbing trees, scrambling through the woods, or creating plays and games with the neighbor kids. I also had lots of collections: stamps, rocks, shells—anything that looked interesting to me. So I got used to being busy and doing lots of things at once....

My grandfather taught me about the land our small ranch was on by telling stories and taking me on long walks. He would point out plants, rocks, and animal tracks, and he would share the history of our land.

No one in my family ever discouraged me from reading, but no one read, either. I grew up watching TV and playing video games. Reading and writing just kind of bore me because....

CHAPTER 2

What Makes an Effective Paragraph?

> Take a few good, deep breaths. Notice your surroundings;
> feel your feet on the floor, your bottom in the chair, your
> hands on the table or desk or in your own lap. Feel good
> about yourself.... Regardless of how the writing went
> today, you suited up and showed up and did the work.
>
> —*Judy Reeves*

PART 1: WHAT'S THE POINT?

If you cannot answer the preceding question, then you are in the right place. First, let's define a **paragraph**. A paragraph is a passage of writing that develops one **topic** and stays focused on that topic (though the topic itself can be discussed for more than one paragraph). The essential ingredients of a paragraph are

- a **topic sentence**,
- **examples**,
- **analysis,** and
- a **concluding thought** and/or **transition**.

A *topic sentence* provides the central topic/idea that the paragraph will be about.

Examples develop and support this central topic.

Analysis explains the significance of the examples; in other words, you tell your readers why and how the examples you have used are helpful.

Finally, *a concluding thought* winds up this topic. A *transition* is a phrase that lets your reader know you are moving on to a new paragraph (and most likely a new topic).

A *paragraph* develops one topic, using a *topic sentence, examples, analysis*, and a *conclusion* and/or *transition*.

THE WRITING PROCESS

Writing is wonderfully *messy*—at any level of preparedness, in any form or context. Unfortunately, we often get trained (and train ourselves) to create "perfect" **drafts** the first time we lay pen to paper or finger to keyboard. Let me remind you: there is NO need for perfection the first time you **compose** any piece of writing. At this point, you are just getting your ideas out; you will have plenty of opportunities to work with all aspects of writing and fine-tuning when you **revise** and **proofread.**

There is no such thing as a "perfect" draft; excellent does not mean perfect.

Various models exist to explain/teach/learn the writing process:

Linear   The linear model of writing is the old standby wherein the composing process is seen as straightforward with a beginning, middle, and end. You compose, revise, proofread, and submit your writing to another reader:

Compose $\longrightarrow$ Revise $\longrightarrow$ Proofread $\longrightarrow$ Submit

Circular   According to the circular model, the writing process circles back on itself at times. You compose a first draft and then revise it; however, you will often come back to composing and revising rather than just doing each step once. Finally, you proofread your final draft, sometimes going back to revise and proofread again. When you are satisfied with content, organization, and sentence-level details, submit it to another reader:

Compose ↻ Revise ↻ Proofread $\longrightarrow$ Submit

Private-to-Public   Both of the above models follow the private-to-public plan, but even in other writing models it is good to keep in mind that you often have a reading **audience** beyond yourself. Your first draft can be written entirely for yourself—just get the ideas out. However, then you move on to addressing the needs of your readers. What do they expect, need, and want to read?

Each model has strengths and weaknesses, and each works for some people some of the time. In fact, each model can work for the same people at different times, depending on what they are writing.

MYTHS AND TRUTHS ABOUT PARAGRAPHS

Myth 1: One topic equals one paragraph.

Truth: When writing paragraphs, you want to keep your reader in mind as you work on both content organization and white space (empty space, like margins and breaks between paragraphs).

Yes, focusing on one topic in a paragraph is important. However, you can use more than one paragraph to discuss one topic. Sometimes, you simply need to give your reader's eyes a rest. *White space* is fine—as long as there is not too much of it (and "too much" varies from context to context).

➤ Below is an example of a paragraph focused on one topic. This is the introduction to an essay that writing student Christina Payson wrote reflecting on an influential part of her childhood. She uses humor by linking her childhood growth phases to different styles of shoes:[1]

> When my mom is talking to people, she notices what color their clothes are. When my best friend is talking to people, she observes what type of jewelry they are wearing. When I am talking to people, I always seem to know what shoes they have on. Maybe it is because I have a shoe fetish and need to buy every pair that fits me. Or maybe it is because feet are the grossest part of the human body and I need to make sure I am a safe distance away from them. Either way, when I look back on my life and my memories, I always remember what shoes I had on. Like everyone, my life is broken up into different stages of trends, views, and morals. So when I was asked to write a personal essay on an educational experience, shoes were the first things that came to my mind. To me, shoes are the strong memory that ties to my personality at a specific time. Through shoes I can easily relate to where and who I was in my life.

➤ Here is an example of several paragraphs that are focused on the same topic:

> When my mom is talking to people, she notices what color their clothes are. When my best friend is talking to people, she observes what type of jewelry they are wearing. When I am talking to people, I always seem to know what shoes they have on. Maybe it is because I have a shoe fetish and need

to buy every pair that fits me. Or maybe it is because feet are the grossest part of the human body and I need to make sure I am a safe distance away from them. Either way, when I look back on my life and my memories, I always remember what shoes I had on. Like everyone, my life is broken up into different stages of trends, views, and morals. So when I was asked to write a personal essay on an educational experience, shoes were the first things that came to my mind. To me, shoes are the strong memory that ties to my personality at a specific time. Through shoes I can easily relate to where and who I was in my life.

KEDS

Any girl who was born in or grew up in the eighties had at least three pairs of Keds. They were the little slip-on tennis shoes with four holes for the shoelaces. They came in every color under the sun, and I had pretty much every one of them: blue, green, pink, red, orange, purple, black, and of course, white. I wore them from kindergarten to second grade. I was quite the little tomboy in elementary school, so my shoes got worn out pretty quickly. My big toe always wore through the canvas, but once this happened, all I would do is take the laces out and I was fashionable once again. My mom never understood this act, and now that I am looking back, I don't either. But I was seven, and all I really cared about was reading as many books as I could so that I could get the free pizza coupons. My life consisted of the typical suburban childhood. I would wake up at six o'clock in the morning for the sole purpose of watching cartoons. School was strictly for physical education and recess. Learning and boys were not a factor—not then anyway. My worlds revolved around *Jem and the Holograms, Care Bears*, and playing hide-and-seek with the neighborhood kids. My worries were shallow or nonexistent.

REEBOKS

At the beginning of every school year, I would get a new pair of shoes. Third grade came along, and with it the white Reebok high-tops with the two Velcro straps at the top of the shoe. These lasted much longer than Keds, and not only were girls wearing them, so were mothers. I thought I was so cool with my fluorescent socks and white tennis shoes. In fourth grade I got the new "double tongues" Reeboks. They were lavender and white. Nothing special, *except* they had an extra tongue that covered the laces when they were tied. New Kids on the Block and slap bracelets were the current trends, and I had my fill of both. My questions were more complex. Why do we really need to know how to write in cursive? And we're in fourth grade now (out of the primary grades), so why does the teacher still feel the need to have the alphabet on the top of the chalkboard? I never would have guessed that the alphabet would still be there in high school. I think I genuinely cared about school because the grades were "real" letter grades, not E+ or S−, and we got to carry a Trapper Keeper binder instead of the school-provided folders. I didn't watch cartoons anymore. I was at a dance or soccer or softball or swim team. That was the period where anything to tire us out would come in handy, to my mom.

➤ Christina continues on this theme, taking us all the way up to college. Although each section is a long paragraph, she could actually split the paragraphs into shorter ones if she wanted to by looking for logical separation points. For instance, one point is between "… my fill of both" and "My questions were more complex." However, each paragraph effectively develops its topic.

➤ Another important note is that all of her paragraphs are connected to the same topic, even though they discuss the topic from different points in time (and from different shoe perspectives!).

Myth 2a: All paragraphs should be short.

Truth: If you have a string of short paragraphs, you will create a machine-gun-like rhythm that can put your readers to sleep. Again, think about variety of presentation as well as organization.

➤ Here is an example of ineffective short paragraphs:

I felt the miles burn away underneath the tires. The freeway pavement was smooth except for an occasional blown retread.

The landscape shifted from ugly to loathsome to downright pathetic. It was mostly cityscapes and junkyards. I don't find cityscapes attractive.

➤ The above paragraphs are split in unnecessary places, simply creating a choppy, undeveloped effect. The reader will want more details. You can create one good paragraph by combining most of the sentences into one passage.

➤ Here is a better version of the above paragraph. (The italics signify text added to make the details a bit more vivid.)

I felt the miles burn away beneath the tires. *The view from the Honda wasn't pretty, but at least I didn't have to worry about streetlights or potholes.* The freeway pavement was smooth except for an occasional blown retread. The landscape shifted from ugly to loathsome to downright pathetic. It was mostly cityscapes and junkyards. *Not a sign of nature was present; all was cement, dust, scrap metal, broken glass, impersonal office buildings, dilapidated brownstones.*

To say the least, I don't find cityscapes attractive.

➤ The second version combines most of the sentences into a longer, more descriptive passage. In fact, this passage can be much further developed with helpful details, specific examples, and so forth. The final paragraph has only one sentence, yet it emphasizes how the driver feels about the surrounding landscape. Here, the emphasis is intended, so the single, set-apart sentence works well. If this were your paragraph, you could continue adding thoughts, details, and images here and there—in other words, *revising*.

Below are two very effective short paragraphs from a children's book entitled *Why Am I Going to the Hospital?*

> Did you ever wonder what you are made of? The stuff inside you?
> Well, you're made of things like skin and bones and veins and blood and organs. (No, not the kind you hear played in church! Organs like lungs and heart and liver, that kind of stuff.) You also have lots of nerves and muscles.[2]

➤ This book is explaining hospitals to children ages eight and younger. If the book were written for college readers, it would read quite differently, wouldn't it?

Myth 2b: All paragraphs should be long.

Truth: Paragraph length can and should be varied. That old cliché "variety is the spice of life" holds true for writing as well as other things. It's important to create thoughtful, well-developed paragraphs, focusing on a topic, supporting your claims with appropriate evidence, and explaining your choices and point of view. But sometimes, for emphasis or clarity, you may want to set off one sentence by itself. Or you may be using dialogue, so you have to create a new paragraph each time the speaker changes. The main point is to do what it takes to effectively develop an idea—and this involves time and practice.

In either of the above two contexts, use *common sense*. If you know you tend to run short, push yourself to write longer paragraphs by developing your ideas. This takes practice. You may find yourself simply repeating the same idea in different words at first, thinking that you're developing an idea when in reality you're just rewriting the same thought over and over again. If you tend, on the other hand, to run long, check your organization carefully and look for places where you can cut out excessive wordiness and/or create paragraph breaks.

Myth 3: A paragraph should be 10–15 sentences long.

Truth: Paragraph lengths vary. Again, use your judgment: if your writing is lean, then writing paragraphs with 10–15 sentences will be a good exercise for you.

➤ Here is an example of an effective paragraph that contains only six sentences. In "How to Tame a Wild Tongue," Gloria Anzaldúa writes about the languages she learned to speak while growing up on the Texas-Mexico border. Although many people reduce them to Spanish and English, Anzaldúa is making the point that there are actually many variations of "one" language. In only six sentences, she manages to get a lot said:

> My "home" tongues are the languages I speak with my sister and brothers, with my friends.... From school, the media and job situations, I've picked up standard and working class English. From Mamagrande Locha and from reading Spanish and Mexican literature, I've picked up Standard Spanish and Standard Mexican Spanish. From *los recién llegados*, Mexican immigrants, and *braceros*, I learned the North Mexican dialect. With Mexicans I'll try to speak either Standard Mexican Spanish or the North Mexican dialect. From my parents and Chicanos living in the Valley, I picked up Chicano Texas Spanish, and I speak it with my mom, younger brother (who married a Mexican and who rarely mixes Spanish with English), aunts and older relatives.[3]

Anzaldúa needs this amount of content to get her point across, which is that her "one" language is actually a multitude of languages. She uses enumeration (a **mode of discourse** that involves listing) to emphasize this point.

Myth 4:   A single paragraph can jump from topic to topic.

Truth: This really becomes a problem for your reader, who will start off thinking you are writing about one particular topic and then suddenly find that the focus has switched without warning. Have you ever listened (or tried to listen) to someone who jumps around from one idea to the next in conversation without completing a thought? Very quickly, this becomes confusing. You end up with no idea what the person's point is. A paragraph that doesn't maintain a focus is just as confusing. What I am referring to is a lack of **unity**. Unity involves an awareness of the primary focus—and stays with this focus.

Unity means that the writer develops one clear focus. He or she does not go off on a tangent or jump around from one unrelated idea to the next.

Here is an example of a non-unified paragraph. The italic type in brackets indicates places that need more development; there are no transitions from one idea to the next:

> My name, Leslie, is Celtic for "from the gray tower." *[How do I know this?]* How depressing—yet kind of cool! *[Why?]* My parents named me after my mother's mother, and strangely enough I resemble her the most of my

relatives. *[Describe this resemblance.]* Lots of people misspell my name, giving it an *-ley* ending. *[How do I respond to people who do this?]*

Here is an example of the same paragraph unified around one topic:

> My parents named me Leslie after my mother's mother, and strangely enough I resemble her the most of my relatives. At least I think so. We both have dark hair, although she had blue eyes and I have green eyes. Our faces are both kind of oval shaped, though not with pointed chins. And we both have serious expressions that completely light up when we smile. There are other physical similarities that I won't go into; let's just say I didn't inherit the long, slender body shape common to my father's side of the family.

➤ Notice how I have picked one focus (resemblance between me and my maternal grandmother) and stayed with it; this is what creates unity. Although the first paragraph's topic is my name, it still shifts from focus to focus (the definition, what I think of the name, resemblance to my grandmother, misspelling the name). This constant shifting can confuse your reader because there is no clear focus or purpose. However, the various focuses can lead to separate paragraphs, which can eventually be developed into an essay.

Myth 5:   If it is all in one paragraph, then you don't have to transition from one point to the next.

Truth: This is a myth that causes many problems. Even though you may be stating your thoughts all in one paragraph, you still have to connect them and transition from one to the next. You also have to transition both within and between paragraphs. Forming these sorts of connections is called **coherence**.

Here is an example of a paragraph with no transitions:

> The first time I wrote my **résumé**, I almost quit my job before I started. I had worked as a food preparer in fast-food restaurants, a clerk in a couple of medical clinics and other offices, and a (terrible) sales representative in a crafts store. I was applying for my first teaching position. At first I was stumped. I decided I needed to look at some models, so I asked several people I knew for copies of their résumés. Each résumé was different. They all gave me ideas. Some of the résumés focused more on the skills that people had learned rather than on the jobs they had held. They listed their jobs. Their résumés focused on major skills and achievements. This made it easier to figure out how I could relate my clerical and sales experience positively to teaching. I could communicate effectively with customers and also research information for them. I could organize a vast amount of paperwork. I already brought some experience with me even though I had never actually been a teacher before.

➤ Even though you can get the basic idea by reading the above paragraph, it jumps around so much that reading it is painful. All the paragraph needs is a few connecting words, punctuation marks, and phrases, and it can flow much more smoothly.

Here is the same paragraph with transitions (in *italics*):

> The first time I wrote my résumé, I almost quit my job before I started. *For about ten years,* I had worked as a food preparer in fast-food restaurants, a clerk in a couple of medical clinics and other offices, and a (terrible) sales representative in a crafts store. *However, now* I was applying for my first teaching position, *and* at first I was stumped. *How do you write a résumé for a type of job you've never had? After some thought,* I decided I needed to look at some models, so I asked several people I knew for copies of their résumés. Each résumé was different, *but* they all gave me ideas. *One thing I noticed was that* some of the résumés focused more on the skills that people had learned rather than on the jobs they had held. They *still* listed their jobs, *but* their résumés focused on major skills and achievements. This made it easier to figure out how I could relate my clerical and sales experience positively to teaching: I could communicate effectively with customers, research information for them, and organize a vast amount of paperwork. *It became clear to me that* I already brought some experience with me even though I had never actually been a teacher before.

By the way, do not panic if you aren't sure about how to use some of the punctuation marks in the above paragraph. Just try them out—and read about how to use them in this and other books about writing. Then try them out some more. Get feedback from other writers. Proofread as carefully as you can, reading aloud to hear how it all sounds. And then try them out some more! Revising and proofreading will help you be more accurate with punctuation because you will be taking the time to check it all out.

PART 2: APPLICATIONS

The following activities will help you think carefully about how audience, language, and content relate to one another. In addition, you will explore what makes different paragraphs effective.

APPLICATION 2–1: Working with Language and Content

Let's look again at that passage from *Why Am I Going to the Hospital?* Remember, this book is written for very young children, probably between the ages of five and eight. Read the paragraphs carefully, doing your best to look at them through the eyes of a child. Then try out my suggestions below.

Did you ever wonder what you are made of? The stuff inside you?

Well, you're made of things like skin and bones and veins and blood and organs. (No, not the kind you hear played in church! Organs like lungs and heart and liver, that kind of stuff.) You also have lots of nerves and muscles.

Now, first list any words and phrases from this passage that seem to be for children:

_____

_____

_____

_____

_____

_____

_____

_____

_____

After you have finished the list, ask yourself *why* these words work better for children than, say, words like "anatomy," "circulatory system," and "epidermis." Answer your question in at least five sentences. (Remember, this is a first draft; don't expect it to be perfect. You will revise it later):

_____

_____

_____

_____

_____

_____

_____

_____

Now, ask yourself *why* the paragraph lengths are appropriate and helpful, considering whom the book is for. Again, answer your question in at least five sentences:

_____

_____

_____

_____

_____

_____

_____

_____

APPLICATION 2–2: Analyzing Paragraphs

Here is a passage from a book introducing formal theories of environmentalism:[4]

For Romantics the excrescences of industrial capitalism were epitomised in the city. Anti-urbanism is a prime feature of romantic thought, as it persists in some ecocentrism today. The Romantic movement reflected a reversed perception of the city, as it did of wilderness. Tuan (1974) shows that the design of the ancient and medieval city made it not only a shrine to God but also an expression of society's highest cultural and technological achievements. This "sacredness" contrasted with the "profanity" of wild nature, as noted above. With the increased importance of industrial manufacturing in the city, however, these positions were reversed, and as the wilderness became sacred, so the city was regarded—especially in Romanticism—as profane.

Yes, the above paragraph seems long and complicated for those of us who are not familiar with the language of formal academic theory. However, its purpose is to introduce adults to theories about the environment. So, what is it doing well? What is it doing poorly? Why? First, let's get the vocabulary out of the way.

Rather than letting unfamiliar words scare you away from reading, find out what the words mean. For instance, "excrescences" means "abnormal developments." How did I figure this out? First, I looked closely at the sentence to see if it could give me clues about what the word means. Second, I looked the word up in a **dictionary** and found a specific definition for it.

Don't let words intimidate you; they are just words. No one is expected to know the meaning of each word in his or her language. This is why we ask questions and look up definitions in dictionaries.

If you hear a word but don't know how to spell it, how can you can look it up in a dictionary? First, ask someone who might know how to spell it. Second, sound out the word slowly and see if you can spell one part of it at a time. Even if you only get the first three or four letters of the word right, that is often enough to get you to the correct section of the dictionary, where you can then look carefully for the word that seems to fit the best.

Below, list the words that you don't yet understand from the environmentalism passage above. If you have a learning disorder like dyslexia, write the word as carefully as possible and then show it to someone to make sure you spelled it right. Also, compare it carefully with the same word in the passage above. Once you have listed the words, find their definitions.

_____

_____

_____

_____

_____

_____

_____

_____

Who do you think the intended **audience** is for the above book? Describe this audience in detail in three to six sentences.

_____

_____

_____

_____

_____

_____

_____

_____

_____

What clues do you have that tell you who the reading audience might be? Write a detailed paragraph that gives examples and explains how the examples are clues.

_____

_____

_____

_____

_____

_____

_____

_____

_____

_____

Based on what you have figured out about the paragraph's audience, what do you think the paragraph does well? Why?

_____

_____

_____

_____

_____

_____

_____

What do you think the paragraph does poorly? Why?

_____

_____

_____

_____

_____

_____

_____

_____

Endnotes

1. Christina Payson, "Walking in My Shoes," (unpublished essay, University of Arizona, 2000), 1–3.

2. Claire Ciliotta and Carole Livingston, *Why Am I Going to the Hospital?* (New York: Carol Publishing Group, 1981), n.p.

3. Gloria Anzaldúa, "How to Tame a Wild Tongue," *Borderlands/La Frontera: The New Mestiza* (San Francisco: Aunt Lute Books, 1987), 56.

4. David Pepper, *Modern Environmentalism: An Introduction* (London: Routledge, 1996), 202.

CHAPTER 3

Audience and Context
Your Reader(s) and Other Influences on Your Writing

> The work I have chosen demands connection,
> not separation.
> —*Nancy Mairs*

PART 1: WHAT'S THE POINT?

Audience and context are two necessary parts of effective writing. Your audience is your readers, and they determine the tone and vocabulary you will use, the information you will impart, and the format you use. Context means the influences on your writing (social, cultural, personal, emotional, psychological, geographical, historical, etc.), and they can come from within or without. Being aware of your audience and the context(s) influencing your writing will help you make connections between your words and thoughts and those who read them. And without this connection, you will have no readers and no purpose for writing.

AUDIENCE: WHAT IS IT REALLY?

Your **audience** is your reader or readers—those people who will not only read your writing but respond to it in a variety of ways. If your readers know nothing else about you, they will get their first impression of you from what you say on paper—and how you say it.

Readers' Ages   Depending on your readers' ages, they will have different interests and concerns: peer pressure, standards of success, relationships, sense of authority, and social pressures. People of different ages also think differently from one another (as can people of the same age).

A five-year-old might be very concerned with finger painting and learning to read; a twenty-year-old might be wrestling with decisions about college, career, and a new relationship; and an eighty-year-old might be interested in a wide variety of topics, having developed many interests over the years.

Each reader will speak and think differently, with varying vocabulary (fairly limited vocabulary in the case of very young readers). They will have grown up with different slang terms and other common expressions. Therefore, you will have to present your material differently to each age group.

Readers' Backgrounds   Age is not the only element that plays an important role in audience. Perhaps the most influential role is played by the readers' backgrounds. How have they experienced the issues, ideas, and experiences that you are writing about? Where you may have positive feelings about something, one or more of your readers may feel negative about it—or vice versa.

And how important is writing to your readers, anyway?

Cultural backgrounds can vary widely even within the same country. If you are from the South, you will have grown up in an environment different from New England or the California coast. What social and cultural influences are strong in your readers' lives? If you don't know the answers to these questions, you risk losing your readers' interest and maybe even their respect.

Readers' Expectations   Readers will have different expectations in different contexts. Here are two general scenarios to give you an idea of what I mean:

1. If you're writing to your parents and your best friend about a particular incident, do you think you will use the same language or reveal the same information in the same way to each audience? It's highly unlikely. Your best friend might be more concerned with all the details, while your parents might be more concerned with your level of responsibility in the matter.

2. When applying for a job, you know that prospective employers will be very interested in your previous job experience and also in any other experiences of yours that are related to the position you're seeking.

There are as many writing contexts as there are written texts, each one with a particular audience that has particular needs and expectations. Again, if you ignore these needs and expectations, then you risk losing your readers' interest, trust, and/or respect (i.e., your *credibility*—or believability—with them).

CREDIBILITY

How believable are you? That is your **credibility**, which is usually shown by how thoroughly you support your ideas and by the tone you use to express them.

Support   **Support** refers to the examples, details, explanations, and interpretations that show why and how an idea is credible. Do you support your main ideas with specific examples? Do you explain *why* and *how* these examples are significant? What do they mean? Why are they important? What other details and explanations do you bring in? If you're leaving a lot up to your readers to figure out, then you're making them work too hard. They won't "fill in the blanks" in the same ways you do, because they don't think exactly like you do. You could also cause your readers to misinterpret your ideas if you leave too many of them unexplained.

> Your *credibility* is how believable you are as a writer. You create or lose credibility with *support* and *tone*.

Tone   How do you sound on paper, and is it appropriate for the particular purpose and audience you are writing to? Your *tone* is the sound of your "voice" on paper; it can sound respectful, pompous, simplistic, encouraging, informative, or patronizing. Make sure it works for your readers.

Tone depends a lot on your word choices. It's good to stretch your vocabulary, but make sure you know that you are using the words correctly. If you don't, this could lead to a lot of embarrassment. You also want to make sure your readers understand the vocabulary you are using. The way you use words sets a mood—formal or casual, for instance.

> Would you expect articles written in *Sports Illustrated*, *National Geographic*, *Maxim*, and *Smithsonian* to sound the same? Even if some of the same people might read each magazine, they will have different expectations of each. *Sports Illustrated*, of course, will focus on sports, athletes, and action—with lots of pictures and a moder-

ate amount of writing. The focuses of *National Geographic* will range from nature to world cultures. It, too, will offer photographs, but they will be blended with quite a lot of writing. *Maxim*, geared toward young men (much as *Cosmopolitan* is geared toward young women), will offer a variety of articles on style, sex, and material success, with lots of advertising that pushes material gain and physical strength and attractiveness. Articles will be brief and generally supported with pictures that reinforce a certain standard of youthfulness and beauty. *Smithsonian* will contain lengthy articles that focus on very specific topics: a style of painting, the history of clock making, Chippendale furniture. The language will be at a college level rather than an eighth- or ninth-grade level.

WAYS OF COMMUNICATING

When you communicate in writing, your readers cannot hear your spoken voice or see your facial expressions and body language. Their clear understanding of your ideas depends entirely on your written words. As a writer, you are helping your readers understand, see, and/or feel what you have written about. As we discussed in the preceding section, your readers' expectations play a huge role in how you write to them. In addition to readers' expectations, your purpose and the form in which you choose to write are very important for effectively or ineffectively communicating in writing to your audience.

Purpose   What is your purpose for writing? The **purpose** is the main reason why a text is written.

For example, the purpose of an argument paper against bringing non-native plants into your neighborhood is to **persuade** your readers not only to agree with you but to change their actions if they have been growing non-native plants.

If you are writing a casual hello letter to a friend, your purpose may simply be to inform him or her about how you are feeling and what you are doing.

The purpose of a recipe is to show your readers a process for preparing a specific dish.

Your **résumé** has the purpose of presenting you in a positive and professional light as well as of informing potential employers of your appropriateness for a job.

Your *purpose* is the underlying reason for your text.

Form **Form** refers to the actual type of document that you write. Many forms of writing exist; here are a few of them:

Letters	Reports	Memos
Songs	Personal Essays	Poems
Research Papers	Stories	Recipes
Contracts		

What you are writing about and *whom* you are writing to determine the form of writing you use. As you can see from the list above, not all documents will work in all situations. For instance, if you are a police officer filling out a police report, you don't want to do it as a personal letter. If you are doing formal research on a specific topic, you won't wish to present the information as a poem.

Paragraphs (or stanzas in the case of songs and poems) are part of all these written forms. Without clear, well-supported paragraphs using appropriate tones, none of these documents will be successful.

CONTEXT: WHAT IS IT?

Context is all the surrounding "stuff" that influences the way you write, what you write about, and how others interpret your writing. Context takes many forms such as historical (time), geographical (place), linguistic (language), external social pressures, internal pressures, and personal or professional environment.

Time   When you write it is during the early twenty-first century, which means you will be influenced by patterns of word use that are true to late-twentieth- and early-twenty-first-century English. For instance, in this chapter I am using language in a way that most of you are already fairly comfortable with, although a word might float in that you are unfamiliar with.

If I were writing in the seventeenth century, my word choices and style would be quite different. Here is an example:

> I think it is agreed by all parties, that this prodigious number of children in the arms, or on the backs, or at the heels of their mothers, and frequently of their fathers, is in the present deplorable state of the kingdom, a very great additional grievance; and therefore whoever could find out a fair, cheap and easy method of making these children sound and useful members of the common-wealth, would deserve so well of the publick, as to have his statue set up for a preserver of the nation.[1]

Jonathan Swift (1667–1745)

Jonathan Swift wrote the above passage from "A Modest Proposal" in the early 1700s—about four hundred years ago—and you will notice that the *language* is used in a style that is quite different from what we see today. He uses many words that we recognize, but he does so in phrases that seem strange to our eyes, for example, "whoever could find out" rather than "whoever could suggest" or, in less formal terms, "whoever could come up with." Words like "prodigious" and "deplorable" are also uncommon today, certainly in essays written for the general public.

Texts in our time often blend lots of images with words. We use technology that makes composing, revising, and proofreading; imaging; and communicating relatively quick and easy. Twenty-first-century writers also produce a wide variety of texts that were nonexistent four hundred (even one hundred) years ago: technical reports, interoffice memos, phone messages, faxes, and computer printouts, to name a few.

People today often live fast-paced lives, with multiple responsibilities and roles. Many college students, for instance, are single working parents—raising families, working full-time jobs, and attending school part- or full-time. Much reading is done on the run, in bits and pieces. However, some of you also enjoy reading longer texts—novels, for example—and want them available to you. And of course in college, you're reading textbooks, essays, scientific reports, mathematical analyses, letters…. The list goes on. And you are or will be writing many of these forms—for your courses and in your personal and professional lives.

As recently as seventy years ago, we didn't have televisions. Books, newspapers, letters, film, and radio were how we got most of our information about various subjects. All of these forms still exist and are used a lot today, but television, video, and computer media have eclipsed them.

Place *Where* you write also greatly influences you. There are government differences, cultural patterns, social manners/mannerisms for different situations, and personal or professional environments (i.e., are you writing a document for work or for personal reasons?).

Let's return to the passage from "A Modest Proposal." Swift was writing in Ireland, then a part of the British Commonwealth (under British control), and he had lived in England as well. Therefore, he was familiar with the social conditions, government, manners, and so forth of these two countries in the eighteenth century (*geography/place*). This familiarity helped him choose the tone and **vocabulary** that would have the greatest impact on his readers.

In college you will find yourself writing many formal documents such as essays, research papers, and technical reports. Some of these you will also write in your jobs. College and work are part of your professional environment, in which much of what you produce will be intended for others to see.

Your personal environment, on the other hand, involves documents like journal entries and letters to friends and family. Some of you keep personal journals, and you know these words probably will not be seen by anyone but you, so you might express more emotions, write incomplete sentences, and jump from thought to thought without worrying about how clear it might be to anyone else. This can be true with a lot of the **brainstorming** you might do for professional pieces, too.

Language As we have already seen with the above passage from Swift, language is influenced by time and setting. However, another issue with language exists: what languages do you think, speak, and write in? Is English your first language, or do you have another first language (Spanish, Mandarin, Russian, etc.)? I have been told by Spanish-speaking students, for instance, that they enjoy reading in Spanish far more than in English simply because "Spanish sounds prettier." Our ears and minds are tuned in to our childhood language(s) in different ways than they are to language(s) we learn later in life.

In college or at work, you might be expected to use language in very formal ways, following strict **format** guidelines for *tone* and vocabulary. When writing for yourself or to a friend, you will often use a more casual tone and vocabulary.

Internal Concerns Finally, when you write, you are also influenced by your internal state of mind: your assumptions, emotional baggage (whether conscious or not), prejudices, beliefs, memories, and experiences.

Again, we'll look at Swift for a moment. He was a well-educated Anglican priest concerned with social problems (like the starvation and homelessness of the poor Irish who could not afford to pay rent to their absentee English landlords). He was angry at the way the upper and middle classes ignored the horrible conditions of the Irish poor, and he had gotten tired of suggesting logical social changes to people who could help the Irish but wouldn't.

All of these experiences and concerns influenced him both from within and without. He was angry, socially conscious, highly religious, very concerned for his fellow human beings, and he believed that no one should live in poverty (*internal influences/pressures*).

What influences you when you write? What might you not even be conscious of unless you think hard about it?

Context has many parts:

Place	Time	Social/cultural influences
Internal influences	Language	

PART 2: APPLICATIONS

In this section, we will work on applying the role of audience in writing. In addition, you will closely explore yourself as an audience.

APPLICATION 3–1:   Paragraphs for Different Audiences

Here are paragraphs from a variety of magazines. Read each passage, deciding which magazine from the list below you think it comes from and why.

Magazines

Smithsonian   *Maxim*

Newsweek   *Sports Illustrated*

National Geographic

You might find it useful to discuss your ideas with others, or if you're working alone, brainstorm some ideas. When you have definite answers, write a paragraph about them.

1. "'Están aquí!' 'They're here! They're here!' someone cried out. It was just after dawn on Saturday. The Miami relatives of Elián González and various of their advisers and hangers-on were awake, or half awake, in the cluttered living room of the small bungalow in Little Havana. Some were sitting around a speakerphone, in negotiations with the Justice Department. Or so they thought, before two federal agents in black body armor jumped the back fence, and eight more burst through the front, firing stinging pepper spray and shouting, 'Get down! Get down! Give us the boy!'"

_____

_____

2. "Want to get really, really close to your favorite hockey star but don't have the connections to get box seats? Why not wear a jersey once worn by a guy who gets paid to bleed? Several companies have recently sprung up to offer game-worn jerseys that still carry the evidence of concussion-inducing checks, kidney-bruising slap shots, and the occasional bout of profuse hemorrhaging."

_____

_____

_____

_____

_____

_____

_____

_____

_____

_____

3. "No one remembers which local clown dreamed up Marysville's trike races. Sometime in the 1970s, a bunch of the regulars who frequented the saloons along State Avenue began racing kid-size trikes around obstacles, stopping to down a beer at each bar. Over the years, the races got bigger and crazier. More obstacles were added. Helmets became mandatory and beer stops were eliminated. Brett Edwards' uncle raced in those pioneering meets, and Brett, a 26-year-old auto machinist, caught the fever. Seven years ago, he built a trike at a cost of $1,500. It has mountain-bike suspension, an aluminum frame and a low, sleek design for cornering. Like any good hot rod, it's painted candy apple red and white."

_____

_____

_____

_____

_____

_____

_____

_____

_____

_____

_____

4. "At the wheel of his new Ford when the 2000 season began at Daytona in February, Rudd couldn't wipe the smile off his face, not even after crossing the finish line on his roof in his first outing, the Bud Shootout, a qualifying run for the 500. 'No regrets,' he says of trying to make it on his own, 'but I don't think I'd want to be an owner-driver again. I never enjoyed the business side of it.'"

_____

_____

_____

_____

_____

_____

_____

_____

_____

5. "Because of its rich mix of people and language and the isolation of the forest people from those on the coast, Suriname is difficult to define. Ninety percent of Suriname's population of 430,000 lives along a narrow strip of fertile land that stretches along the Atlantic coast. Here people of African and European ancestry live alongside the descendants of people from China, India, and Indonesia. Tolerance is the rule, and marriage between groups is common."

_____

_____

_____

_____

_____

_____

_____

_____

_____

_____

APPLICATION 3–2: Identifying Audiences through Tone and Vocabulary

Look at a magazine or journal that interests you and see if you can figure out the exact audience it's written for. Look at its tone and vocabulary as well as the subject matter. Do the same with a film, a web site, and/or a book.

A **magazine** is written for a general audience. It has lots of pictures, advertising, and sometimes very little written text. The language is often at about a seventh- to ninth-grade level. A **journal** is written for a specific audience of experts in its particular subject. It contains little or no advertising, few (if any) pictures, lots of written text, and bibliographic references. The language is at a college level, and it is assumed that the readers have college educations. Both magazines and journals are **periodicals**, which simply means that they're published periodically throughout the year (weekly, monthly, quarterly, etc.).

APPLICATION 3–3: Identifying and Analyzing Audiences for Advertisements

Locate an advertisement in a magazine or newspaper. Who do you think is the intended audience? What clues from the advertisement help you identify its audience? Write a paragraph answering the above questions and beginning with a topic sentence. You can brainstorm (see chapter 5) at first to generate ideas and examples.

_____

_____

_____

_____

_____

_____

_____

_____

_____

_____

_____

APPLICATION 3–4: Identifying and Analyzing Audiences for Coupons

Locate a coupon in a magazine or newspaper. Who do you think the intended audience is? What else is the coupon "selling" besides the product? How is the coupon presenting the product? Write a paragraph answering the above questions and beginning with a topic sentence. You may first do brainstorming (see chapter 5).

_____

_____

_____

_____

_____

_____

_____

_____

_____

_____

_____

APPLICATION 3–5: Describe Yourself as an Audience

1. Your Characteristics and Environment

Your family:

_____

_____

_____

_____

_____

_____

_____

_____

_____

Your age: _____

The community you grew up in:

_____

_____

_____

_____

_____

_____

_____

_____

Cultural influences:

_____

_____

_____

_____

_____

_____

_____

_____

_____

How you learned to read and write:

_____

_____

_____

_____

_____

_____

_____

_____

_____

_____

2. Your Interests

Your hobbies:

_____

_____

_____

_____

_____

Social situations you are comfortable in:

_____

_____

_____

_____

_____

_____

Types of reading and writing you like:

_____

_____

_____

_____

_____

3. How might all of the above characteristics and backgrounds have influenced what you like and don't like to read and write?

_____

_____

_____

_____

_____

_____

_____

_____

_____

4. What would make a writer seem credible to you?

_____

_____

_____

_____

_____

_____

_____

_____

_____

_____

APPLICATION 3–6: Rewriting a Paragraph

Rewrite the passage from "A Modest Proposal" in present day language and style.

Here is the passage for you to refer to:

> I think it is agreed by all parties, that this prodigious number of children in the arms, or on the backs, or at the heels of their mothers, and frequently of their fathers, is in the present deplorable state of the kingdom, a very great additional grievance; and therefore whoever could find out a fair, cheap and easy method of making these children sound and useful members of the common-wealth, would deserve so well of the publick, as to have his statue set up for a preserver of the nation.

Below is a space for your rewrite, if you would like to use it. Otherwise, use a sheet of notebook paper or your journal.

_____

_____

_____

_____

_____

_____

_____

_____

_____

_____

_____

APPLICATION 3–7: Different Languages for Different Writing Purposes

For those of you who use more than one language, which language(s) do you use for which types of writing? Why?

_____

_____

_____

_____

_____

_____

_____

_____

_____

_____

_____

APPLICATION 3–8: Analyzing an Advertisement

Find an advertisement that advertises a diet plan or formula using a female model. How does the ad present the woman? What part(s) of her body does the ad focus on? Is what you see moving from "fat" to "thin"? What is the ad implying about how the ideal woman should look? Is it selling anything in addition to a diet or fat-reduction formula? What about the plan or formula itself—is it made to appear to work like magic? What cultural influences are at work here?

Below or on a separate sheet of paper, an audio tape, or whatever works for you, identify the ad you chose, and include it with your final draft. Answer the above questions, supporting your answers with specific examples from the ad. You don't have to write an organized paragraph at first, but once you get your ideas out, begin organizing them into a thoughtful, detailed paragraph that has a clear and interesting topic sentence.

_____

_____

_____

_____

_____

_____

_____

_____

_____

_____

APPLICATION 3–9: Analyzing a Magazine Cover

Select and study a magazine cover. Who is the intended audience? How is the cover designed to appeal to that audience? What subjects are presented on this cover? How are words, colors, and images presented? Which words and images are larger, and which are smaller? Is the cover designed effectively to appeal to the magazine's intended readers? Why or why not?

_____

_____

_____

_____

_____

_____

_____

_____

_____

_____

_____

_____

Endnote

1. Jonathan Swift, "A Modest Proposal," Project Gutenberg. 10 August 2001. ftp://ibiblio.org/pub/docs/books/gutenberg/etext97/mdprp10.txt (1997.–Modest Proposal, A–Urbana, Illinois (USA): Project Gutenberg. Etext #1080.–First Release: Oct 1997–ID:1107)

CHAPTER 4

Reading and Writing *Are* Connected

When you want to write in a certain form … read a lot of
writing in that form…. When you read a lot in that form, it
becomes imprinted inside you, so when you sit down to
write, you write in that structure.
—Natalie Goldberg

PART 1: WHAT'S THE POINT?

Reading and writing influence each other directly in
many ways. The more you read, the more you see words and
phrases in action and expand your vocabulary. In addition,
you are exposed to a variety of styles, from very simple to
very formal, and a variety of readers. All of this exposure will
make you a more flexible writer, one able to work with and
create many different documents effectively. Reading a variety of works will increase your awareness of your own language, style, subject matter, context, and readers—and how
they all work together.

WHY DO READING AND WRITING RELATE TO ONE ANOTHER?

Well, when you write, you are also reading; otherwise, you wouldn't be able to make sense of the words. And you certainly would have no idea whether your readers would be able to make sense of them!

UNDERSTANDING CLEAR WRITTEN EXPRESSION

If you can see it as a reader, then you are aware of what you need to do as a writer. Think back to the first few times you were learning to read and write. Your teachers had you write out letters, maybe begin memorizing the alphabet and experimenting with spelling and putting any old words together. At the same time, they were reading to you and encouraging you to read. The first books were probably fairly simple, with one or two short sentences and lots of pictures to a page, but you were seeing words in action to form meaning, even as you were learning to do the same thing on paper yourself.

Here is an example from my childhood:

When I was six years old, my first-grade teacher read *Fun with Dick and Jane* to my classmates and me. Dick and Jane were a white boy and girl who lived in the suburbs with their dog, Spot (and Mom and Dad, of course). Mom stayed home and Dad went to work at the office every weekday. This was supposed to be a typical family, but soon after my first-grade year, the book wasn't used anymore because a lot of people finally realized that it was *not* describing a typical family, just a stereotype. Anyway, the sentences read something like this:

"See Jane run."
"See Dick throw the ball."
"See Spot chase the ball."

We would match the words to the pictures and slowly get a sense of what the different words meant and how sentences were formed.

Kids growing up in the 1990s had books like *Is It Dark? Is It Light?*[1] read to them.

One page has an illustration of a steaming mug of cocoa and a dish of ice cream. The underlying caption states, "Is it hot? No it's cold."

Although from different generations, we are all faced with the processes of matching words to pictures and forming sounds from letters.

We also worked on our letters, and eventually on spelling. I was given long sheets of lined paper to write on. The lines were about an inch apart, so I had plenty of room to work with. Slowly and painfully, I would write out letters of the alphabet, looking at the strip of alphabet paper that was pinned over the blackboard and wrapped around the classroom walls: a big "A" and a little "a"; a big "B" and a little "b." Finally, I'd get to spell my first name.

All of this took time—days and weeks—but slowly I learned that what I wrote was the same sort of thing that I was learning to read in books: words and thoughts on paper; ideas that people were trying to communicate to other people.

OTHER BENEFITS OF READING

Reading also expands your **vocabulary**, knowledge of **grammar** and **punctuation**, sense of **style**, and general knowledge base (your awareness of various subjects, types of documents, and so forth). The more you read, the more words you see and begin to understand. Sometimes you might not be sure what a word means, but if you look at the sentence or phrase that it's in, you can at least guess at the meaning and check it in a dictionary later.

You will also be exposed to a variety of grammatical constructions and punctuation marks, seeing, for instance, how apostrophes are (and are not) used or how plural subjects and verbs agree (see pages 117, 121). For example, I learned how to use a colon (:) (see page 117) by seeing it used in books and magazines; that was what helped me understand the rules for colon usage that I had read about in high school.

A sense of style is harder to put into words, but basically it means knowing when words are and are not flowing together smoothly. Are sentences clunky or unclear? Are there too many short sentences that begin to sound in your head like a machine gun going off? Is the same word repeated over and over instead of a variety of words? These are examples of awkward style that can quickly lose the attention of any reader. If you develop a strong eye for style, you will begin to put words, phrases, sentences, and paragraphs together in effective ways, and your readers will stick with you.

Another benefit of reading is simply that you see lots of different document types: books (novels, textbooks, etc.), essays, news articles, web sites, contracts, letters (formal and informal), memos, e-mail notes, lists, and on and on. This gives you a much larger variety of texts to choose from when you are writing. It also allows you to get comfortable reading a large variety of texts and understanding their different uses. This way you know what document is best for what situation, just as you will have a clearer sense of what tone, style, and vocabulary are best for each writing situation.

All of this gives you a lot of flexibility—as a reader, writer, and general communicator in all areas of your life.

PART 2: APPLICATIONS

In this section you will begin leaning to determine what documents are best for different writing and reading situations. In addition, you will explore how reader expectations influence the content and style of various documents.

APPLICATION 4–1: How Would You Write About...?

Below are some writing situations. Think carefully about each situation and decide what type of written document would be best for it. Then write or talk about why a particular document would work best in a particular situation. Finally, write a sample document for one or more of the situations.

Document	Why Document Works
Renting an apartment or buying a house.	
Applying for a job.	
Telling a story to a ten-year-old.	

Document	Why Document Works
Advertising a sale of young adults' clothes.	
Describing how a baseball is made.	
Showing how Martin Luther King's "I Have a Dream" speech influenced the Civil Rights Movement.	
Notifying your boss that you have finished a project.	

APPLICATION 4–2: What Would You Want as a Reader From ...?

The above boxes describe only a few writing situations. Writing is used in so many ways that sometimes you may not even be aware of it. For example, a lot of us might not think that mathematics and writing go together, even though we see that they do every time we open a textbook, take a math test, or write notes about a mathematical formula.

In the same way, you are reading for different reasons at different times. When you read a recipe, for instance, you are looking for a series of steps to follow in order to successfully prepare and cook something. When you receive a letter from a friend, you expect it to be personal and to refer to people, situations, feelings, and other information that you can relate to.

Look at each of the boxes above again, but this time as a reader. Ask your-self what you would need to know from each document. Here are some questions you will have to answer as a reader:

How would you want that information presented to you (i.e., what kind of written document)?

What specific information would you want/need?

Use your answers to fill out the chart below:

	Document	Specific information needed
Renting/buying a home.		
Telling a story to 10-year-olds.		
Advertising young adults' clothes.		
How a baseball is made.		
MLK's "I Have a Dream" speech.		
Reading that your employee has finished a project.		

Once you have completed the chart, choose at least one of the topics to write a paragraph about, using the above questions to help you.

_____

_____

_____

_____

_____

_____

_____

_____

_____

_____

_____

APPLICATION 4–3: **Forms of Prose Style: How Does Reading a Certain Kind of Document Help You Write a Certain Kind of Document?**

Each piece of writing that you read is written in its own particular **prose** style. By *style*, I mean the **tone** and vocabulary used and the way the sentences are written. Style can be "plain," "middle," and "formal."

Plain style generally involves very simple words and short sentences. It is not incorrect, but it can be quite limiting because a lot is being left out of what is written. Here is an example of plain style:

> Jake rode his red bicycle.

Middle style still uses language that most readers can understand, but the vocabulary is more sophisticated. Sentences tend to be longer and have more variety; however, again they are quite clear to most readers. This book, for instance, is written in middle style.

Formal style involves vocabulary that not as many readers will understand. The tone can appear distant, sometimes arrogant (but not always). Often, it is written to fellow experts in a subject who know the jargon. You will also see this style in formal invitations and many upper-division college textbooks (particularly theoretical books). Here is an example of formal style:

> The preponderance of questionable motives hints at an irregularity in the defendant's credibility; however, we will leave the issue of guilt for a jury to decide.

The **context** within which a text is written greatly affects its style. Letters between two close friends will probably be written in plain or middle style. A college research essay will probably be written in middle or formal style (unless the writer is not paying attention to his or her audience). Understanding the best style for any writing situation involves understanding people's expectations within that situation. But becoming familiar with a range of prose styles also depends on the variety and number of writings you *read*.

Carefully read the writing samples below, one at a time. You will probably be able to decide quite easily which prose style each excerpt uses. Once you have decided on the prose style, write a paragraph explaining why you think it is that particular style and use specific examples to support your explanations. In other words, *show* your readers what led you to your conclusions.

First writing sample:[2]

My name is Marie Wilson and I am the director for the White House Project, an organization that breaks through barriers against female leadership. Fellow women, I am here today to talk about women in politics. Women's needs are not being met, and your voices are not being heard. We have won the right of suffrage, but we are not using it wisely. There are 535 members in the House and Senate, and out of these there are only about 70 women representatives. Over half of the U.S. population is comprised of women, and there are only 30 representatives. This demonstrates that we are not exercising our right to vote. We fought long and hard to win the privilege of voting, and now we are not using it to its full potential. We need to rise up as one and demand our fair share. We need to elect more women representatives and encourage more women to run for elections.

Second writing sample:[3]

For Romantics the excrescences of industrial capitalism were epitomised in the city. Anti-urbanism is a prime feature of romantic thought, as it persists in some ecocentrism today. The Romantic movement reflected a reversed perception of the city, as it did of wilderness. Tuan (1974) shows that the design of the ancient and medieval city made it not only a shrine to God but also an expression of society's highest cultural and technological achievements. This "sacredness" contrasted with the "profanity" of wild nature, as noted above. With the increased importance of industrial manufacturing in the city, however, these positions were reversed, and as the wilderness became sacred, so the city was regarded—especially in Romanticism—as profane (Tuan 1971).

Endnotes

1. Mary D. Lankford, *Is It Dark? Is It Light?* (New York: Alfred A. Knopf, 1991), n.p.

2. Erin Henderson, "Rights for Women" (unpublished essay, University of Arizona, 2000), 1.

3. David Pepper, *Modern Environmentalism: An Introduction* (London: Routledge, 1996), 202.

CHAPTER **5**

Invention
Strategies for Getting Started

How to generate writing ideas, things to write about?
Whatever's in front of you is a good beginning. Then
move out into all streets. You can go anyplace. Tell me
everything you know.
                                           —Natalie Goldberg

PART 1: WHAT'S THE POINT?

Invention is the general process of discovering your
ideas, what you want to write about, and how you want to
write it. It can take the form of **brainstorming**, also called
prewriting, or can be a part of the actual composing process.
The wonderful part of invention is that it allows you to get
your ideas out without following any rules or worrying about
how "good" your writing is. You can generate many ideas,
images questions, and observations that you can later sort
through, organize, delete or develop. Invention, in other
words, helps you move beyond the blank page.

BRAINSTORMING

By now you have some familiarity with the **drafting** (writing, **revising**, **proofreading**) process. Many of you have discovered that you need to come up with ideas for writing before you even begin a first draft, let alone revise a draft. This process of generating ideas is called *brainstorming*. When you practice writing in each chapter of this book, you have the opportunity to brainstorm, which takes many forms, as you will see below.

Brainstorming allows you to come up with ideas quickly without stopping to wonder whether they are all usable. You don't care at this point whether all of your ideas make sense; what you do care about is getting them on paper. Lots of times, once you have jotted words and phrases down, you begin to see connections and patterns that you weren't aware of before.

You don't need to take a long time to prewrite; often five or ten minutes at a time is adequate. It is perfectly all right to brainstorm for twenty or thirty minutes too, though. The main thing is to brainstorm without stopping for at least a few minutes so that you get some thoughts onto paper, on tape, into pictures, or expressed in some other way to help you visualize and organize your ideas.

LEARNING STYLES AND INVENTION

Some forms of invention do not involve writing, and you may find these helpful. If you learn and generate ideas better by talking, by moving, or by imagining them as pictures, some of the ideas in this section might work best for you when brainstorming.

ORAL BRAINSTORMING

Taping   Record your ideas on a tape recorder and play them back later when you want to write them down.

Talking   Talk to other people about your ideas.

Reading Aloud   Read your writing aloud to hear how the words and ideas connect to each other.

Background Noise   Play music or the TV in the background as you write; go to a coffee shop, mall, library, park, or other comfortable public place to write.

VISUAL BRAINSTORMING

Drawing   Draw your ideas out in pictures so that you can visualize them.

Note Cards   Write on multi-colored note cards so you can shuffle them around and reorganize your ideas.

Blocks   Use different colored blocks (each color representing a separate idea) to organize and shuffle information around.

KINESTHETIC (MOVEMENT-BASED) BRAINSTORMING

Compose and Move   Compose your ideas while you walk, ride an exercycle, swim, use a treadmill, or do any other physical activity that helps you organize your thoughts.

Change Positions   Sit at one side of a table to work on one idea, and then move to the opposite side of the table to work on a different idea.

WRITING-BASED BRAINSTORMING

Listing   When you **list**, you simply write down any words that come to mind regarding a certain topic or idea (such as *movies* in this case). After you finish listing, you can then reorganize the list into related ideas/topics. This is just one way to get your ideas out without trying to compose complete sentences. It's very useful for many people.

Movies	Film
Cinema	Actors/actresses
Art films	Bizarre films
Directors	John Waters
Cecil B. Demented	Social commentary
Satire	Genres
Drama	Horror
Ghost stories	*What Lies Beneath*
Science fiction	Action
Action heroes	Jackie Chan
Arnold Schwartzenegger	Comedy

Clustering   When you create a cluster, you write the central topic or idea in the middle of a sheet of paper and draw a circle around it. Then write down any other words and phrases that you think of, whether they seem to make sense or not. Draw circles around these words and phrases, too. Connect related circles to one another with lines to help you begin organizing them. (See the figure.)

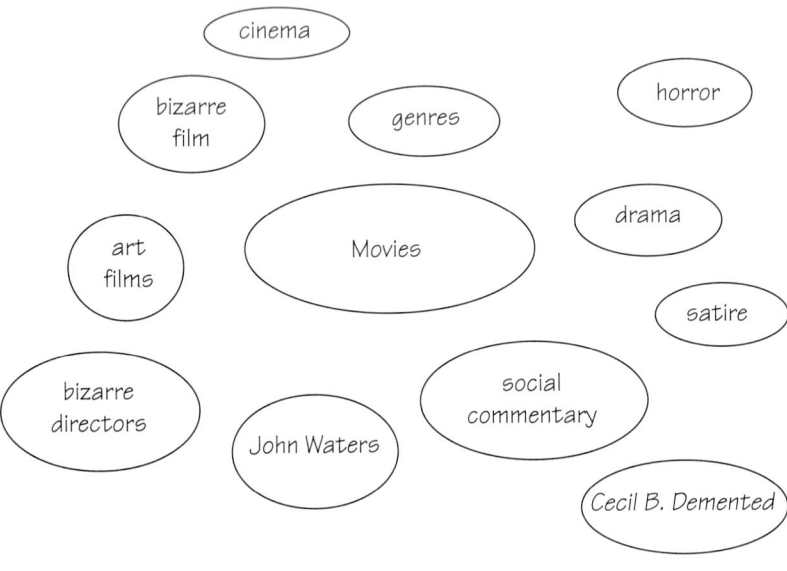

Clustering is a visual way to brainstorm and eventually connect ideas.

Freewriting   When you **freewrite**, you simply pick a time limit (5–10 minutes is a good start) and begin writing. Just let the ideas flow—even if they don't seem to make sense. If you don't know what to write, you state "I don't know what to write" until more ideas come to you. The main thing with freewriting is that you do not stop writing, even for a second. You write continuously for the entire allotted time. Sometimes you might want to write for longer than 5–10 minutes. This is fine; just pick a time limit that works for your writing situation.

Some of you may wonder how freewriting is helpful. Well, what you do is free up your subconscious (which is full of ideas) to bring various thoughts up to conscious mind. Often, your thoughts will begin to connect, but even if they don't, they will usually lead to a useful idea, theme, or topic. When you freewrite, you keep your conscious mind from getting in the way, criticizing, questioning, getting caught up in spelling, and so forth. When your mind gets caught up in the little details or in wondering if what you're writing makes sense, you can quickly lose track of your ideas. Freewriting helps you stay on track.

Here is an example of a freewrite:

> Well, my teacher wants me to write something, but I don't know what to write. Hmmm. What if I write about something I'm interested in—more interesting for me. I don't want to be bored doing this. I love gardening. A lot of people would think this is stupid. But I love it—have always loved it. And I have a yard to try out new ideas. Roses. They've been a pain. But I went to a nursery and asked someone who knew what he was talking about to help me. I wanted roses that would perform well in my area of the country—not easy since it's the desert. But he showed me several and I picked out two and they're doing great. One's lavender the other is deep pink/red. Well, whatever. What do I write? I don't know what to write. Well, um, roses. What about herbs? I love plants that have good and strong scents. I love getting home and wandering through my garden. Of course there aren't many plants yet but there will be in time. Okay, whatever.
>
> Um ... oh it's time to stop.

In the above freewrite, the writer was given no topic, but as you can see, she found one as she kept writing. Now she can continue to explore the general topic of gardening or the more specific ones of roses or herbs in a focused freewrite.

Focused Freewriting   **Focused freewriting** simply means that you choose a word, term, or idea (such as "movies") and freewrite about it for a certain length of time. Again, you're not stopping yourself; you're just getting ideas out—ideas that you can pore through later.

Here is an example:

> Movies. I love going to them every Friday night because I can relax and forget my responsibilities for a while. But I don't want anything too serious. I mostly like action and monster movies—people laugh when I tell them this because they think I'm so serious about so many other things. It is funny, I guess, but it's for relaxation. I've always loved monster movies—even the old 50's creature features. *Them. The Deadly Mantis. Day of the Triffids. The Blob. The Giant Gila Monster. The Brain That Wouldn't Die.* So many of them. I just find them entertaining. And hilarious sometimes. I don't have to take anything seriously but can just drift with the story. I can watch them over and over again—yeah, I know, weird. But not. Instead of football or basketball or other subjects, I watch monster movies to escape. How did I get on to this topic anyway? Well, duh, I picked it. But not monster movies. Hmm. It might be fun to write about them. I could watch them and pick out scenes that I like and explain why I like them—or don't like. I could read about them, which would be fun. I—

Here the writer had a focus but still didn't know where she would end up. But the focus helped her stay within a certain topic area. And she found something she wanted to explore more thoroughly.

Outlining   Outlining is a different type of invention. It is really a way of organizing your ideas from general to specific.

The way an outline works is to separate ideas into broader and narrower topics.

- The broadest topics are marked by Roman numerals (I, II, III, IV, V, etc.).

- Topics that help develop the broadest topics but are narrower are marked by capital letters (A, B, C, D, etc.).

- Narrower topics and/or examples that support the broader topics are marked by regular numbers (1, 2, 3, etc.).

- You can even get more detailed, moving to the next level, which would be small letters (a, b, c, etc.).

As you can see, an outline can be as broad or as narrow as you make it. Each level, however, should have at least two items.

Let's go back to the focused freewrite on movies and pick one topic from it. (Note: In this case, the Roman numeral "I" is designating the paragraph topic. You can also write your topic sentence here. Because we're only working on one paragraph, I'm only using one Roman numeral. If you were to move on to a new topic and/or section, you would designate it with a "II.")

   I. Stopping Alien Monsters

    A. The Blob

      1. Acidlike jelly

        a. Dissolves people and animals

        b. Squeezes through small spaces

      2. Stopped by a simple process

        a. Doesn't like cold

        b. CO_2 fire extinguishers freeze it

    B. Day of the Triffids

      1. Carnivorous plants

        a. Survive on blood

        b. Deadly spray

2. Stopped by a simple process

    a. Water dissolves them

    b. Couple trapped on island spray plants with sea water

Each level down gets more and more specific. You can also discover new ways to organize your ideas. For instance, notice that a new focus has appeared in the above outline: simple processes to destroy alien space monsters. You could now write a new outline with that as the main focus.

Outlines help you organize and prioritize your ideas and support them with detailed thoughts and examples.

You can make your outline as general or detailed as you want to. Do what works for each writing situation, but remember that the more specific your outline is, the easier it will be to compose a first draft.

INVENTION DURING THE COMPOSING PROCESS

Sometimes even when you are writing your first draft, you don't realize exactly what you want to say until you have written several sentences. You may find that you are four or five sentences into your paragraph (or several pages into your essay, when you get to the essay stage) before your writing begins to smooth out, become detailed, and have a point.

At first, it can feel frustrating to look at all the writing you did up to that point, knowing that you have to take it out, but if you are willing to discard the part that doesn't work, you will have a much stronger piece of writing. This is normal; experienced writers also have to get rid of what doesn't work. You can always save the discarded section in a "discard" file on your computer or write it down on a separate sheet of paper. You never know when you might want to use it in other writing.

You can also stop and brainstorm at any point in your writing process. If there is a section in your paragraph that you are not sure about, leave it alone and do the rest; then you can come back to that part later and brainstorm about it for a few minutes.

Remember, you can *brainstorm* at any point in your writing process.

PART 2: APPLICATIONS

In the following activities, you will learn many invention strategies and will have the opportunity to practice them for your own writing.

APPLICATION 5–1: Freewriting about an Advertisement

Locate and study an advertisement for five or ten minutes, and then freewrite about it for at least five minutes and see what ideas you generate.

_____

_____

_____

_____

_____

_____

_____

_____

_____

_____

APPLICATION 5–2: Focused Freewriting about an Advertisement

You can also do a **focused freewrite** on the above ad. There are a couple of ways to do this: (1) you can find a theme/topic in the freewrite you just did and use it as your focus; (2) you can look at the advertisement again and choose some detail in it to write about. Write your focused freewrite for five to ten minutes; you may use the space below if you would like to.

_____

_____

_____

_____

_____

_____

_____

_____

_____

_____

_____

_____

_____

APPLICATION 5–3: Creating a Cluster

Here are some topics. Choose one topic from the list or decide on a topic of your own and do a cluster on it. (Refer back to pages 61–62 if you want to refresh your memory about clusters.) Then, choose a focus from the cluster and write an outline for a paragraph on this focus. (Think about how long and detailed you want the paragraph to be and whether you might even want to write more than one paragraph.)

Fighter pilots	Coffeehouses
Growing container vegetables	Holidays
Poetic images	Family communication styles
The Winter Olympics	Babysitting
Baking brownies	Driving a tractor
Favorite novels	Childhood stories
Watching baseball	Big Brothers/Big Sisters
Playing ice hockey	Playing in a band
Pit bulls	

Cluster:

APPLICATION 5–4: Identifying a Focus from a Cluster

Choose a word or phrase you wrote down in the cluster in the above application, and do another cluster using this word/phrase as the focus. Doing a focused cluster will help you organize a paragraph around a central but manageable topic.

Focused Cluster:

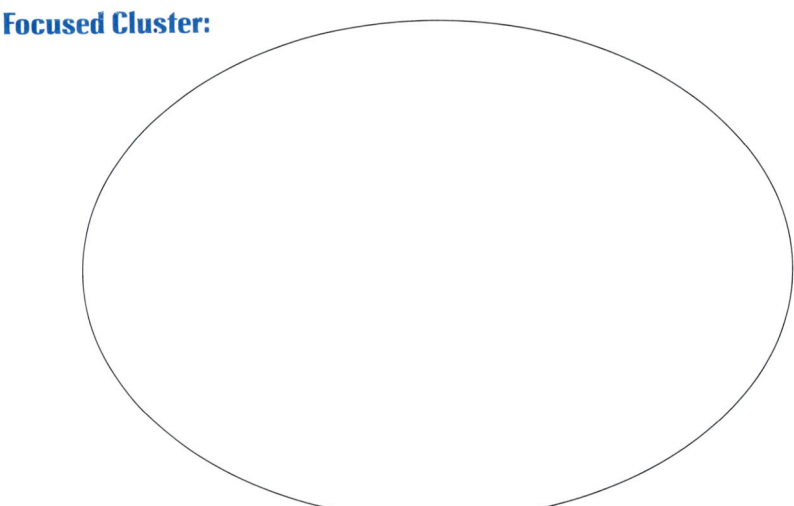

APPLICATION 5–5: Creating an Outline

Create an outline for a paragrah that you are working on. (Refer back to pages 64–65 to review outlining.)

_____

_____

_____

_____

_____

_____

_____

_____

_____

_____

CHAPTER **6**

Making Meaning

Language is more than words. Language is music and rhythm; it is sound, rhyme, and sibilance; it is texture and layers. Art and graffiti. Language is attitude and place, geography and history. Language is family and what you heard at the kitchen table and on the back porch, muffled behind closed doors and shouted up from stairwells. Language is what you do with words and it is the silence between the words.

—Judy Reeves

PART 1: WHAT'S THE POINT?

Making meaning has to do with the words you use, the way you arrange/organize your writing, **focus**, and **unity**. How well you pull all of these ingredients together is how well your readers will understand what you are trying to tell them. Now that you have been **brainstorming** and exploring ideas, you want to make sure that you write about them clearly.

WORDS: DENOTATION VS. CONNOTATION

Words have dictionary definitions (called *denotations*) and emotional meanings (called *connotations*). All this means is that a word has some sort of general meaning, but you may associate something positive or negative with it, too, shifting its general meaning.

For instance, the word "budget" may simply be defined in the dictionary as a financial plan; however, if you have trouble managing your money or you don't always have enough money to meet expenses, "budget" can suddenly have a lot of stress attached to it. Therefore, someone may suggest to you that you budget your money, and you might want to punch him or her in the nose. Suddenly, a word that may have no particular emotional connections for one person has a lot of emotional baggage for another.

> *Making meaning* involves word choice, unity, and organization to convey your ideas to your readers.

A **dictionary** gives you the objective definitions of words. What kind of book can sometimes help you with the connotations? A **thesaurus**. A thesaurus lists words that are similar in meaning to one main word—but the other words often have different *connotations*. So before using a word from a thesaurus, *always* check its exact meaning in a dictionary.

> **Denotation** means the dictionary definition of a word. **Connotation** means the emotional associations you might have with a word because of your life experiences.

UNITY

Unity means how tightly your ideas are connected. Are they clearly related to one another? Something is unified when all of its pieces form a seamless whole. This is not always easy. You want to consider the following questions:

- Are you contradicting yourself?

- Are you losing focus, straying into other topics/ideas that may not belong in this particular paragraph?

- Does the idea you bring up in one sentence *transition* smoothly to the next sentence?

Here is an example of a paragraph that does not have unity:

> Shakespeare's plays sometimes intimidate people who are unfamiliar with the old English words he uses. *Romeo and Juliet* is probably one of the best known romances. Many actors, including women, yearn to play the lead role in *Hamlet*. Some of Shakespeare's phrases are still commonly used today, but people do not realize that the words come from his plays....

You can see the problem. Each sentence in this paragraph brings up a new idea—a new focus. The writer will get lost with so many different topics to discuss; the reader will get lost, too, not knowing what's coming next. Clearly, what the writer needs to do now is choose one focus and stay with it.

Now here is a more unified version of the above paragraph:

> Shakespeare's plays sometimes intimidate people who are unfamiliar with the old English words he uses. His plays were written during the late sixteenth and early seventeenth centuries in Elizabethan England, and many readers find the unfamiliar, older English words and phrases confusing. However, a number of Shakespeare's phrases are still in use today; it is just that we do not always realize we are using them. Phrases such as "it's Greek to me," "tongue-tied," "vanished into thin air," "refused to budge an inch," and "my own flesh and blood" illustrate what I mean....

As you can see, this paragraph stays focused on one idea. It also moves smoothly from one point to the next, slowly developing that idea. This connectedness is *unity*.

Topic Sentences   The **topic sentence** is generally the first sentence you see in a paragraph. It gives you the paragraph's focus, sets the tone, and informs you of the writer's purpose (i.e., *why* the writer is choosing this focus).

What is the main point of your paragraph? That is its *focus*. You create the focus with the *topic sentence*. If a paragraph does not have a topic sentence, it has no organizing framework and can be very confusing. This is because the writer might jump from idea to idea with no focus or plan, so the reader can't figure out what the point is. You also can refer back to the topic sentence when composing and revising, just to make sure you are on track.

If you look back at the second version of the Shakespeare paragraph, you will notice that its topic sentence is clearly stated:

> Shakespeare's plays sometimes intimidate people who are unfamiliar with the old English words he uses.

This is a manageable focus for a well-developed paragraph or two. Referring back to the topic sentence will help the writer remember that his or her focus must remain on the language of Shakespeare's plays.

When you create a topic sentence, think about whether it is manageable in a paragraph or two. In other words, if you write something like, "Gardening is hard work but fun," or "I like basketball," you're setting up a topic that is much too broad. Another problem is that you're creating a very simplistic topic that will probably bore both you and your readers.

You can write about any topic, but you want to make sure that what you write about is meaningful to you. You also want to think carefully about what is and is not important for the particular focus you have in mind.

A general paragraph on gardening is not going to interest many readers, even if they like gardening; however, a paragraph that explores the connection of gardening to creativity might catch your readers' attention. Therefore, a topic sentence like, "The best way for me to express my artistic side is to garden," adds more character and possibility to what you will write. You can narrow this focus even further in order to write a manageable paragraph without trying to cover too much. "Working with herbs has allowed me to experiment with cooking," might intrigue some of your readers enough to read on and find out what you do in the kitchen.

In the same way, writing, "I like basketball," is only going to cause your readers to say, "So what?" However, if you have a topic sentence such as, "Basketball has improved my ability to work through algebra problems," your readers are going to be curious. How can playing basketball make a person better at math? Well, you'll go on to tell them, explaining in general and showing with specific examples how math and basketball are connected.

Transitions   **Transitions** are a very important part of unity. A transition marks a change or shift, letting your reader know that you are moving from one point to another but also showing your reader how you are making the connection between the two points.

Transitional words help you signal that you're moving from one idea to another. These words also show the relationship between the two ideas; therefore, if you do not understand what the transitional words mean, you can create a relationship in your writing that does not make sense. (By the way, "therefore" is a transitional word.)

Here is an example:

> Chuck ran that marathon in forty-seven minutes; furthermore, he's a full-time student at our community college.

There's a problem here because "furthermore" indicates that the writer will be expanding on the first idea rather than introducing a new focus. But the writer does introduce a new focus, which will confuse his or her readers.

Here is a more appropriate use for "furthermore":

> Chuck ran that ten-mile marathon in forty-seven minutes; furthermore, he has run other marathons at an equally amazing pace.

Now that the two ideas are connected, the use of "furthermore" makes sense.

Here is a sample paragraph using highlighted transitional words, followed with an explanation of the words' meanings and uses:

> *Argument* refers to the reasons or logic you offer. Sometimes you may be able to prove conclusively that your solution is best. Sometimes your reasons may not be as strong, the benefits may not be as certain, and obstacles may be difficult or impossible to overcome. For example, suppose that you wanted to persuade your organization to offer a tuition reimbursement plan for employees. You'd have a strong argument if you could show that tuition reimbursement would improve the performance of marginal workers or that reimbursement would be an attractive recruiting tool in a tight job market. However, if dozens of fully qualified workers apply for every opening you have, your argument would be weaker. The program might be nice for workers, but you'd have a hard job proving that it would help the company.

The words highlighted in gray are transitional words. They carry an idea along and help it develop. They also signal to the reader a shift in the idea. "Sometimes" is repeated; it is also used to briefly describe strong and weak arguments. "For example" is used to let the readers know that a specific example is coming up that will demonstrate a situation in which someone's argument can be strengthened. Finally, "however" emphasizes what could weaken the person's argument and develops the central idea that sometimes arguments may not be as convincing as they first appear. These are a few ways words are used to move (transition) from one idea to the next.

Common Transitional Words and Phrases

Although	Consequently
Furthermore	Hence
However	In addition
In other words	Indeed
Instead	Moreover
Nevertheless	Therefore
Thus	

ORGANIZATION

Organization is also a part of maintaining a smooth flow in your writing. If your ideas jump around, they need to be organized—pulled together. Organization works closely with unity, but where unity involves ideas connecting to one another, organization involves the order in which ideas are written.

For instance, are ideas prioritized from general to specific so that a main topic is supported by specific examples? Are related ideas connected to one another or scattered about haphazardly? Does each paragraph have a clear topic sentence?

Your entire paragraph may be unified around one topic, but if you leap around from point to point, not clearly developing one idea before moving on to another one, your readers will become quickly lost. Organization is the basic structure of your paragraph: what comes first, second, third, fourth, etc.

Outlining   A brainstorming technique that works well with organization is outlining (see pages 64–65). An **outline** moves you from your main point (topic sentence) to supporting points and examples. It will also show you when you have scattered ideas around that really belong together.

PART 2: APPLICATIONS

In the activities below, you will be asked to work with topic sentences and transitional words to create unified paragraphs that develop topics and flow smoothly.

APPLICATION 6–1: Topic Sentences

You are now familiar with what a topic sentence is, and it's time to begin practicing. To refresh your memory, a *topic sentence* establishes a paragraph's central focus/main idea.

Write a short list of topics, at least five. They can be as general or specific as you want at this point.

_____

_____

_____

_____

_____

_____

_____

_____

Choose one of the above topics and write at least four topic sentences for it:

Topic	Topic Sentence

Explain why you think you could or could not write a well-developed paragraph from each topic sentence.

Topic Sentence	Why It Will/Won't Work

APPLICATION 6–2: Personal Chart of Transitional Words

Create your own chart of transitional words, but don't just list them without definitions. You need to know what they mean and do, so write short definitions for each word.

Transitional Word	Definition

APPLICATION 6–3: Paragraph

When you have the transitional words in the above application listed and defined, write a paragraph that uses at least three of them:

_____

_____

_____

_____

_____

_____

_____

_____

_____

_____

_____

APPLICATION 6–4: Peer Review

Once you have written a paragraph in the above application that uses transitional words, show it to another writer. Have that person (1) tell you whether the transitional words make sense and (2) replace the transitional words you used with words from his or her list (or of his or her own choosing).

_____

_____

_____

_____

_____

_____

_____

_____

_____

_____

_____

APPLICATION 6–5: Unifying Your Writing

Choose a paragraph from your own writing. Highlight ideas that do not seem to belong with the focus. Explain why they don't belong.

Highlighted Idea	Why It Does Not Belong

Replace the highlighted ideas above with ideas that do belong with the focus. Explain why the new ideas work better.

New Idea	Why It Belongs

APPLICATION 6–6: Creating a New Paragraph

Rewrite your paragraph in Application 6–5 using your new ideas:

_____

_____

_____

_____

_____

_____

_____

_____

_____

Show the first paragraph and the rewritten paragraph to another writer and ask him or her to compare the two, explaining to you which paragraph works better and why.

_____

_____

_____

_____

_____

_____

_____

_____

_____

CHAPTER 7

Revision and Content Development
Getting from the First Draft to the Final Draft

Be specific. Don't say "fruit." Tell what kind of fruit—"It is a pomegranate." Give things the dignity of their names.
—*Natalie Goldberg*

PART 1: WHAT'S THE POINT?

Revision is what you do after you write a first draft. When you compose your first draft, you are just getting the ideas down. When you revise, you go back over the draft, adding important details, taking out unnecessary words and phrases, making sure the topic sentence is clear, and smoothing out organization so that ideas flow smoothly and logically from one to the next. You also look at how you're using words and whether they create clarity or confusion. Areas to look at closely when you revise are **organization**, **style**, and **content development**.

ORGANIZATION

A paragraph's **focus** is established by its **topic sentence**, so first make sure your topic sentence is clear. Then, see if your ideas flow logically from one to the next or if they jump around (which they can do in a first draft because you're just getting ideas out, but which they should not do in later drafts).

STYLE

Style is how you actually use words to get your ideas across. Part of style is **phrasing**, which is how you put words together in a sentence. Have you ever been told your writing is awkward? This means that you need to go back over your word choices and your phrases and rewrite them more smoothly, which takes practice.

How vivid are the words you use? Are words specific or vague? Are you using the same word(s) over and over, or are you varying your **vocabulary**?

Sometimes, you can create what's called **wordiness**. This means unnecessary repetition or using many words where one or two will work just fine. Here's an example of what I mean:

Wordy: The thesis of the proposal was incredibly and amazingly lengthy.

Revised: The proposal thesis was too long.

Excessive wordiness is not the same thing as thoroughness or appropriate length. *Never* just put in words to stretch out the length of your paragraph; your readers will see what you have done because there will be a lot of unnecessary clutter in your writing.

Look for places where you can combine sentences and delete extra words and phrases that do not add anything to your writing. **Punctuation** can be very helpful with this (see chapter 9), especially commas, semicolons, and colons. Here are some examples:

Wordy: She wanted a lot of stuff for her birthday. What she wanted was clothes, makeup, and perfume.

Revised: She wanted a lot for her birthday: clothes, makeup, and perfume.

Wordy: David was in charge of the marathon. He was in charge of selecting and getting approval for a race site and road clearance and police support. And he was also in charge of making sure the racers knew where to go to sign up and get their numbers.

Revised: David was in charge of the marathon; he selected the race site, arranged for road clearance and police protection, and set up an area for runners to sign in and pick up their numbers.

Watch out for "which," also. A lot of writers are not sure how to use constructions like "in which" or "to which." Casual spoken English often uses "which" constructions incorrectly, too, so be careful not to write in the same offhand way as you may speak. All of us speak much more casually than we need to write, especially in more formal writing situations.

Incorrect: Matt grabbed the box in which the china was packed in. *(Notice the extra—and unnecessary—"in" at the end.)*
Revised: Matt grabbed the box in which the china was packed.

See how all the revised sentences flow so much more smoothly?
A helpful web site that links to many other sites on style and usage is *Freelance Writers: Style Guides* at http://techwriting.about.com/cs/styleguides/.

REVISING A PARAGRAPH

Below is a paragraph written by a young man about cooking. I explain and demonstrate revision steps that will improve it; then I demonstrate a revised version.

FIRST VERSION
I got interested in cooking when I started to know the basics. I started boiling water and started putting ingredients together because when I could do some recipes, I was just happy. Knowing I could cook some stuff. And I started cooking vegetable casseroles because they have vegetables and I like casseroles a lot. And then meat dishes. There fun.

➤ Many things are going on in this paragraph; *revision* is needed for *content, organization, style,* and sentence-level errors.
First, the *topic sentence* is quite general, and a lot of readers won't even know what the writer means by "the basics." People who aren't even interested in cooking might skip this paragraph entirely, and even those who are willing to read the paragraph will want much more information. So perhaps the topic sentence can be rewritten something like this:

I got interested in vegetarian cooking when I was ten and my parents let me help them prepare a holiday dinner.

Now, we have a more concrete and focused topic sentence, and the rest of the paragraph will develop and support what is mentioned in that sentence.
What do you think the main focus is? Well, learning to cook vegetarian is part of it, but the topic sentence also makes it clear that the writer's interest developed when he was helping prepare a holiday meal. So now the readers' expectations are set up; they will expect to read about the holiday-dinner preparations and also to be *shown* clearly how these preparations created interest for the writer.

Second, the ideas in the paragraph are not developed well. It's hard to imagine exactly what the writer went through—good and bad—in learning how to cook vegetarian. The paragraph needs main points that develop the context of holiday-dinner preparations; it also needs clear and detailed **examples** that really *show* the readers what's going on.

I keep emphasizing the word "show" because when you write it's important to remember to *show* your readers, not just tell them. Give them details that will help them connect with you and what you're writing about and picture what's being discussed. This will help their understanding and also keep their interest. For example, the writer here could begin with boiling water, chopping vegetables, etc. Then he could move on to preparing traditional vegetable casserole, spinach lasagna, etc. For both examples, the writer should describe his parents, his feelings, his thoughts, and his actions.

Third, the writer also needs to *revise* for *organization.* Is the "meat dishes" sentence appropriate here? This sentence gets the reader off track because it doesn't relate to the main topic. Clearly, the writer didn't prepare any meat dishes for this first *vegetarian* dinner. What this sentence does is branch out from the paragraph's focus into a new focus. The writer needs to either discard it or move it somewhere else where the topic will be useful. If the writer decides to move it, then here are a couple of suggestions:

1. The writer can perhaps conclude his paragraph with a reference to expanding his cooking skills to meat dishes when he got older.

2. The writer can begin a new paragraph with this topic, helping to develop an essay about his cooking experiences in general.

Fourth, the writer also needs to examine his *sentence structure* and *word choices.* He has an unnecessary *sentence fragment.* A sentence fragment is an incomplete thought, phrase, etc., that can't stand alone as a sentence but is made to do that anyway: *Knowing I could cook some stuff.* This is simply a phrase describing the writer's state of mind, but it doesn't offer a complete idea. The rest of the idea is in the last part of the preceding sentence, which can be combined with this one: *I was just happy knowing I could cook some stuff.* The real problem is that "I was just happy" is tacked onto the end of the preceding sentence, but it doesn't belong there. It belongs here, beginning the next sentence. Another fragment is *And then meat dishes.* It's just a phrase that's referring to a new idea, but the idea isn't fully developed, so the reader is left thinking, well what about meat dishes?

Sometimes, however, fragments are created deliberately by writers for emphasis, but they are doing this to create an effect, an emphasis. You will see in the second paragraph draft an example of this kind of fragment. See if you can find it and figure out why the writer used it.

Fifth, a sentence-level error exists for the writer to clean up, too. He writes *There fun.* Technically, this is a complete sentence: *They are fun.* It has a subject and a verb, and that's all that's needed to create a complete sentence (or an independent clause). However, "there" is not the correct contraction for "they are"; "they're" is. This kind of cleanup work can be taken care of during the final stage—proofreading; however, if the writer notices it while revising, it's a good idea for him to make the change at that time.

One way you can revise is to read the draft aloud to yourself, putting check marks in the margins beside places where you hesitate (even if you are not yet sure why you're hesitating) and beside places you know will need improvement. Reading aloud will help you hear your writing in a new way. Once you've read your essay aloud, go back to the beginning and read it silently, marking any other areas you think may need improvement. After this, you might want to put the paragraph aside again for a day and then return to it and begin making changes that improve it.

Here is a tip for revising style. Reading aloud can be very helpful in catching awkward style because you can't fill in the blanks as easily as you can when reading silently.

Here is the second version of the paragraph on page 83, showing much improvement:

SECOND VERSION

I got interested in vegetarian cooking when I was ten and my parents let me help them prepare a holiday dinner. Dad pulled a vegetable carving knife out of the narrow drawer under the counter. For years, he had warned me not to use this knife because it was so sharp, and I felt a surge of pride as he placed it in my hand. The knife! I was holding it—this amazing blade that would transform the colorful pile of vegetables waiting to be sliced and chopped. My mom handed me a huge beefsteak tomato, and I began carefully slicing it as they both watched quietly but alertly. After the tomato was sliced, I was handed an onion. My eyes filled with tears as my knife cut into it, and I remembered watching my parents cut onions and wondering why they cried. Now I knew! Dad heated the wok on a gas burner, adding olive oil, which began steaming after a few seconds. Mom helped me scoop the onion pieces into the hot pan. After about fifteen seconds, the air was fragrant with cooking onions, and I helped my parents add garlic, tomatoes, and asparagus to the mixture. I was given the job of stirring the whole thing, knowing I was responsible for keeping it from burning over the high heat. I was just happy knowing I could finally contribute to this important family meal. My parents and I laughed at the mess and talked about everything— what I was doing in school, our vacation plans, what we'd each like to give others over the holidays, how we wanted to decorate our house. When the vegetables were beginning to soften a tiny bit, my mom helped me pour them into a casserole dish. To this mixture, we added five kinds of cheese and two eggs (we ate dairy products), thoroughly stirring it all together. We topped the casserole with crumbled homemade croutons, which would brown and form a buttery tasting crust, and placed the whole thing in the hot oven. I couldn't wait, not only because I loved casseroles but because I had helped make this one. I'm twenty-five now, and I still love making and eating casseroles. They're fun.

This second draft is much more detailed than the first draft, but more revision can be done. What can be revised? Well, more concrete (specific) words and vivid details can be added. The writer might also want to change the ending. In addition, other examples might either work better than or be a helpful addition to the examples already included. In the next revision, the third version, changes are highlighted:

THIRD VERSION

I got interested in vegetarian cooking when I was ten and my parents let me help them prepare a holiday dinner. Dad pulled a vegetable carving knife out of the narrow drawer under the counter. For years, he had warned me not to use this knife because it was so sharp, and I felt a surge of pride as he placed it in my hand. The knife! I was holding it—this amazing blade that would transform the colorful pile of vegetables waiting to be sliced and chopped. My mom handed me a huge beefsteak tomato, and I began carefully slicing it as they both watched quietly but alertly. After the tomato was sliced, I was handed an onion. My eyes filled with tears as the knife sliced into it, and I remembered watching my parents crying as they cut onions. Now I knew why they cried! Dad heated the wok on a gas burner, adding olive oil, which began steaming after a few seconds. Mom helped me scoop the onion pieces into the hot pan. After about fifteen seconds, the air was fragrant with cooking onions, and I helped my parents add garlic, tomatoes, and asparagus to the mixture. I was given the job of stirring the whole concoction, aware of my responsibility to keep it from burning over the high heat. I was just happy knowing I could finally contribute to this important feast. My parents and I laughed at the mess and talked about everything—what I was doing in school, our vacation plans, what we'd each like to give others over the holidays, how we wanted to decorate our house. When the vegetables were beginning to soften a tiny bit, my mom helped me pour them into a casserole dish. To this mixture, we added five kinds of cheese and two eggs (we ate dairy products), thoroughly stirring it all together. We topped the casserole with crumbled homemade croutons, which would brown and form a buttery tasting crust, and placed the whole thing in the hot oven. I couldn't wait, not only because I loved casseroles but because I had helped make this one. I'm twenty-five now, and I still love making and eating casseroles. They're fun.

You can also see that this paragraph is getting quite long. It is okay to have a long paragraph that thoroughly develops and supports its focus. If you ever feel like it's getting too long—like you will lose your reader if you don't give his or her eyes a rest—then find a logical place at which to separate it into two paragraphs. The second paragraph doesn't need a topic sentence because it's really just a split from the first paragraph.

OTHER WAYS TO REVISE

There is a variety of ways to help you revise your writing, some of which do not immediately involve writing. If you learn and think more easily in pictures, by talking, or by moving, here are some tips that you can apply to your revision process:

- Read topic sentences aloud.

- Begin work with visual information—videos, slides, photos, etc.

- Color code information on different-colored note cards or with different-colored pens.

- Read key parts of your sources aloud whenever possible.

- Draw charts.

- Picture ideas in your mind.

- Use audio tapes, narrated films, lectures, and other sources with sound.

CONTENT DEVELOPMENT

Content development means that you *thoroughly* support your ideas rather than just making one statement and moving on to the next one. It will help you a lot to temporarily (or just in your mind) insert "because" at the end of every statement you make; doing this will force you to explain your ideas completely. You can also ask *why* something is the way it is or *how* it got to be that way. Asking *why* and *how* forces you to explain yourself carefully.

If, for instance, you are writing a paragraph about liking a certain model car, do not just stop at saying you like it. You also have to *show* your readers why and how this particular car fits your needs and expectations. This means that you not only explain why you like it (e.g., it's easy to drive, economical on gas, and has no maintenance problems) but also provide examples so that your reader can really see what you mean. Once you provide those examples, explain how and why they support your claims.

WHO IS/ARE YOUR READER(S)?

If you have no awareness of your readers as you write, then you are not thinking of the people (audience) who will be reading your words. This can be a big problem because when we write only for ourselves, we leave a lot of holes, filling in the blanks from memory and personal experience. But your readers don't share your memories, experiences, or ways of thinking. They might have no idea what you are trying to say, especially if you leave out important details and other information—or if your writing is unclear in any other way. Below is an example of what I mean.

➤ This passage is based on a powerful essay written by a young man about a near-death experience he had. During this experience, he "dreams" that he is talking with his grandfather, who reassures him that all will be well. Below is the concluding paragraph, discussing his attitude change after he recovers; however, I've removed certain information, which I will put back later:

> When I awoke almost a week later, I was in a hospital room. The first words I spoke were, "I talked to Papa Ray." My mom began to sob. As soon as she finished crying, she told me that I had been in a coma for six days. After that experience, I looked at life differently; my grandfather's powerful words ("always persevere no matter how hard life gets...") began to guide me and give me a new philosophy about life.... Because of him I got the strength I needed to overcome all obstacles in my path....

➤ The places above that have the ellipses (...) are marking passages that I have deliberately left out. Look at the above paragraph again. The writer makes important points: that his life changed and that he developed a new philosophy about life. But without any other information, his readers are left wondering exactly *how* his life changed and *what* his new philosophy became. He hasn't yet filled in the blanks for them. If this were your paragraph, you would now want to give some examples that let your readers in on your experiences, and this is what the writer does in the completed paragraph below (inserted material is highlighted):

> When I awoke almost a week later, I was in a hospital room. The first words I spoke were, "I talked to Papa Ray." My mom began to sob. As soon as she finished crying, she told me that I had been in a coma for six days. After that experience, I looked at life differently; my grandfather's powerful words ("always persevere no matter how hard life gets...") began to guide me. His words make me feel protected and watched over. Because of this I have opened up to people more, gotten involved in outside activities, and felt strong enough to face my health problems. Papa Ray's words also gave me a new philosophy about life. I began to work harder in school and pulled my grades up. I played baseball and felt healthier and more self-confident. Success in school and athletics encouraged me to keep trying. Because of him I got the strength I needed to overcome all obstacles in my path....

➤ The highlighted words help complete the writer's story. They explain enough to his readers so that they can begin to really picture how his life and attitude changed. (This, of course, also makes us want to know more about what was going on—an example of the power of reading and writing.) What you have just seen is *content development*, a way of adding important information to help your readers see what you mean and to make sure you are communicating with them clearly.

Now the writer can keep adding specific details to develop the paragraph further until it clearly shows his triumphs and personal growth.

THOROUGHNESS VS. PARAGRAPH LENGTH

Sometimes you may find yourself worrying about how long your paragraph "should" be. Do not be tempted to just put in filler words. (A *filler word* is a word that takes up space but doesn't add anything important to your writing; it's just used to make the paragraph look longer or to substitute for a more substantial idea.)

Instead, look at how you can develop your ideas.

- Are they supported thoroughly?

- Have you explained how and why the examples represent what you mean?

➤ Below is a paragraph written with a lot of filler words but very little idea development (of the *topic sentence*):

The news reporter interviewed four members of the jury, and the interviews were filmed for our journalism class. This was the reporter's version of the right questions to ask in a news interview. I could see right from the start that she had done a lot of research on the trial and was well prepared to ask the jury members questions about it. Her questions were thoughtful and right for the situation. She came off as being respectful, and her body language was polite as well.

➤ At a quick read, the above paragraph may seem complete, but when you read it more closely, you can see that a lot of information is missing or just replaced with filler words. For instance, what was the reason the interviews were filmed for the journalism class? What questions did the reporter ask? How could the viewer tell from the questions that the reporter had done a great deal of research?

➤ The writer says that the questions were "thoughtful and right for the situation," but what does that really tell us? We still have no idea what made them "thoughtful" and "right" because we are given no specific information (no examples of her questions). Finally, the writer notes that the reporter's behavior was respectful and her body language was polite. There are two problems here. First, once again we have no specific information to help us understand "respectful" and "polite" in this situation. Second, the sentence is redundant: "came off as being respectful" and "body language was polite" are both really saying the same thing. In addition, "come off" is a slangy **colloquialism** that takes away from the paragraph's professionalism.

Here is the same paragraph with stronger *idea development* (in the highlighted text) rather than just general or repetitive filler words and phrases:

> The news reporter interviewed four members of the jury, and the interviews were filmed for our journalism class in order to give us a good model. This was the reporter's version of the right questions to ask in a news interview. I could see right from the start that she had researched the trial thoroughly and was well prepared to ask the jury members questions about it. Some of the questions were simply about the jurors to get background information from them. For instance, she asked them where they worked and if they had ever been on juries before. Other questions were directly related to the trial. Her question about the use of the defendant's family background by his defense lawyers was insightful. Her questions were thoughtful and appropriate for the situation. Her manner was assertive yet respectful. She made sure that each person she interviewed answered all of her questions, but she never raised her voice, interrupted, or bullied anyone. When someone had trouble answering a question, she would restate it so the person had a clearer idea of what she meant. She also never shoved her microphone right into anyone's face; instead, she held the microphone about four inches in front of whoever was speaking. All in all, we had a very effective interview model to work with.

➤ This paragraph can still be smoothed out and cleaned up, but it has greatly improved from the first version. Now, at least, the reader is being given information that's specific enough to show what the writer means.

If you are convinced that you have developed an idea as much as you can, yet the paragraph is still short and lacks information, you may need to write a broader topic sentence. Sometimes the first topic sentence does not work out as well as you think it will. That's okay; just write another one. This is what revision is all about; it allows you to try something out and, if it doesn't work, to try something else.

DEVELOPING IDEAS VS. SIMPLY REPEATING THEM

If you are new at content development, you may find yourself wondering how to do it. This is perfectly natural; all writers struggle with content development at some point. You might find that you simply write an idea over and over in different words, thinking that you're developing it when you're really just repeating it.

➤ Here is an example of a writer simply repeating the same idea over and over again:

> Chinese society had a rigid pyramid structure, with the emperor at the top. The most powerful man was the emperor, and he was more powerful than anyone else. Everyone else was below him in rank, from his advisors to the common people....[1]

➤ Here the writer is confused between actually developing an idea with new ideas (which is how it's supposed to be done) and restating the idea several times (which is how many of us start out).

In fact, the above paragraph was not what the writer used in the book. Here is the actual paragraph, taken from a children's book on world mythology.

➤ The paragraph explains how the pyramid structure in earlier Chinese society is reflected in Chinese myths (stories that try to explain mysteries of life). These extra explanations also help the readers to visualize what the writer means by "pyramid":

> Chinese society had a rigid pyramid structure, with the emperor at the top. In Chinese myths, Heaven and Hell are structured in a similar way. There was a mythical king in charge of Hell, with ten judges and courts of Hell below him. A mythical emperor—known as the Jade Emperor—was in charge of Heaven and also presided over the courts, judges, and officials. On Earth, the emperor was called the "Son of Heaven" to show that he was connected with the hierarchies of Heaven.

Ways to develop an idea:

- Use examples.
- Explain how the main idea relates to some other idea.
- Compare the main idea to something else, which is called **analogy**. For example, in the above paragraph, the emperor is compared to a god.

PART 2: APPLICATIONS

Revision and content development are essential for creating thorough paragraphs. In this section, you will have the opportunity to expand on your paragraph topics and supporting ideas and to incorporate and discuss relevant examples. These activites will also help you learn to distinguish between developing your ideas and merely repeating them in different words.

APPLICATION 7–1: Using Analogies

Yikes! What's an *analogy*? It's simply a comparison of one thing to another. An example would be comparing an athlete's physical training to army boot camp. Here, the analogy is between disciplined physical exercise and a highly structured, disciplined army environment—lots of sweat in both of them! This analogy gives you a clearer idea of how hard the athlete must work to train for competitive sports events. Army boot camp is traditionally full of hard work, long hours, lots of strenuous physical and mental activity, and little control over one's life—in other words, lots of hard work.

The list below presents a variety of topics. Come up with a brief analogy to describe each one. You can write your answers on the blank lines here, or in your journal or notebook.

■ Fishing on a small pond in the middle of August

_____

_____

_____

■ Sailing on the ocean

_____

_____

_____

■ A salmon's experience swimming upriver to spawn

_____

_____

_____

■ Walking through a museum

_____

_____

_____

■ Watching a football game in the stadium

_____

_____

_____

■ Watching a football game on television

_____

_____

_____

■ October in New England

_____

_____

_____

■ July in Arizona

_____

_____

_____

■ Waiting for your first paycheck

_____

_____

_____

■ Studying for final exams

_____

_____

_____

■ Siamese cats

_____

_____

_____

APPLICATION 7–2: Paragraph

Write a paragraph that develops one of your analogies in Application 7–1. First, write a topic sentence; then work from there. See how you do, what's hard and what's easy, and then talk about it with your classmates.

_____

_____

_____

_____

_____

_____

_____

_____

_____

_____

_____

APPLICATION 7–3: Supporting Examples

Again working from the list in Application 7–1, write examples that develop at least one topic.

Topic	Examples

APPLICATION 7–4: Paragraph with Examples

Now write a paragraph using some of the examples you chose in Application 7–3. Don't worry about getting it perfect; just get your ideas on paper:

_____

_____

_____

_____

_____

_____

_____

_____

_____

_____

APPLICATION 7–5: Style: Cleaning Up Your Sentences

Select five sentences from your own writing and revise them to clean up wordiness and awkwardness. Choose the most awkward, lengthy sentences you can find! Otherwise, you will not get much practice. Do this sort of activity whenever you revise your writing for style, reading sentence by sentence to make sure your ideas are clear and smoothly written.

Sentence 1

Original version:

_____

_____

_____

_____

_____

_____

_____

_____

Revised version:

_____

_____

_____

_____

_____

_____

_____

_____

Sentence 2

Original version:

_____

_____

_____

_____

_____

_____

_____

_____

_____

Revised version:

_____

_____

_____

_____

_____

_____

_____

_____

Sentence 3

Original version:

_____

_____

_____

_____

_____

_____

_____

_____

_____

_____

Revised version:

_____

_____

_____

_____

_____

_____

_____

Sentence 4

Original version:

_____

_____

_____

_____

_____

_____

_____

_____

Revised version:

_____

_____

_____

_____

_____

_____

_____

_____

_____

Sentence 5

Original version:

_____

_____

_____

_____

_____

_____

_____

_____

Revised version:

_____

_____

_____

Endnote

1. This passage is altered from Cynthia O'Neill et al., eds., *Goddesses, Heroes, and Shamans: The Young People's Guide to World Mythology* (New York: Kingfisher, 1994), 111. The original passage is reproduced on page 91.

CHAPTER 8

Working on Your Paragraphs

> ... I go on telling people to consider finding someone
> who would not mind reading their drafts and marking
> them up with useful suggestions.... There are probably
> a number of ways to tell your story, and someone
> else may be able to tell you whether or not you've
> found one of those ways.
>
> *—Anne Lamott*

PART 1: WHAT'S THE POINT?

Seeing your writing as useful and public strongly affects your sense of authorship. You become accountable when you know someone else will be reading your work. You also gain a better idea of how clearly you are communicating your ideas to other people—and also how accurate your sense of audience is. You see your writing in a variety of contexts and get a good sense of its usefulness. Seeing other people's writing lets you see new models, other strengths and weaknesses. It also gives you more objectivity and a better perspective to practice working with your own and other people's writing.

There are several ways to work with your writing, among them **portfolios**, **workshops**, and **peer evaluations**.

PORTFOLIOS: GATHERING YOUR BEST WORK

In a portfolio, you select three or four (or more) pieces of your writing over a period of time—a semester, a month, a year, whatever. You can choose what you consider your best work, or you can show work that moves from weaker to stronger. It is a great way to follow the growth of your writing.

Portfolios have many uses. Sometimes teachers use them to evaluate your coursework and assign a grade. Sometimes portfolios are used to apply to schools and for jobs. They are also a great way to organize your writing so that you have old and new models to look at. In addition, you can include writing that has been commented on by someone else, a teacher or a peer. These comments might offer advice that is helpful to you in future writing.

WORKSHOPS
In the Classroom

- The classroom is a safe place in which to share your work with peers and see their work, too.

- You can fill out forms, read aloud, draw pictures of your ideas, and discuss each other's writing—no one is singled out.

- **Critiques** are specific and helpful, pointing out strengths and areas that need **revision**.

Reading aloud is very helpful when you are working with others or yourself. When you read your own writing aloud, it is easier to hear awkward phrasing, places that are missing important information, sentences that run on and on, and other grammatical and stylistic errors. This is because you actually *hear* your words rather than silently skimming over them.

Outside of the Classroom   *Online*—The benefit of working online is that you can read and post responses and critiques on your own time or while you are working in a convenient place. In online settings, people can post writing samples, and group members and/or all classmates can post responses. People can also post responses to earlier responses. In other words, working online allows you great flexibility in communicating to others about your writing.

Small-Group Meetings—When you meet outside of class in small groups, it can feel more private and relaxed than it might be in the classroom. You can meet at coffee shops, the library, parks—any place that works for the group. As in any other workshop situation, you follow the same basic peer-evaluation procedures.

ONE-ON-ONE PEER EVALUATION

One-on-one peer evaluations are simply when two people work intensively on each other's writing. You can do this in person, in writing, or both. One of you can read aloud while the other looks on at a copy of the same paragraph. Both of you can exchange paragraphs, each quietly reading the other's work and taking notes (preferably on the actual draft). You can also write a detailed memo or letter to one another, citing specific strengths and areas for improvement and using examples from the person's own writing. And you can talk to each other about your writing.

Here are sample questions that peer evaluators can address in their comments:

- What is the **topic sentence**?

- Is the topic sentence clear?

- What is the paragraph's **focus**?

- Is the **organization** clear? Logical?

- Is the writer developing ideas or just repeating them?

- Are the ideas interesting and complex? Why or why not?

- What **examples** does the writer use?

- Do the examples support the main points in the paragraph?

- Is there a concluding statement? What does it say? Why does it work or not work?

- Would you like to see other examples in addition to or instead of those used? What examples would you like to see? How would they improve the paragraph?

- Are there explanations of what the examples mean? Do these explanations make sense?

- How unified are the ideas?

- Is there any awkward phrasing?

- How could awkward statements be rewritten?

- Are words used incorrectly or carelessly?

- Are words or ideas repeated unnecessarily?

- Are there any major grammatical errors (sentence fragments, singular/plural disagreement, etc.)?

When peer-evaluating, you may also look for typographical errors (typos) and spelling, punctuation, and format errors. You do not have to fix them; just circle them. If you notice an error pattern (e.g., the writer keeps using a comma when a semicolon is needed), circle only one or two and point out the pattern to the writer. This way the writer can learn to look for and clean up the error pattern him- or herself.

PART 2: APPLICATIONS

The following activies will introduce you to a wide range of evaluation techniques for your writing. They cover both individual and peer evaluation strategies; you will work with others to give them feedback on their writing and to receive feedback on your own writing. You will then analyze the feedback and incorporate appropriate comments into your revision.

When you discuss your own and other people's writing, be honest about what is and isn't clear to you and why. If you're too vague, then you won't be helping anyone (including yourself) improve his or her writing.

APPLICATION 8–1: Portfolio

Choose three to six of your paragraphs and put them together in a *portfolio*. Revise and proofread these paragraphs. You may even write a cover letter that introduces them and explains their various strengths and/or any other reasons why you have included them.

One of the most important, and often most neglected, phases of the writing process is revision. When you revise, you go deeply into your written document and work on several levels. You look at how thoroughly the content is developed and whether or not it relates to the topic sentence. *(Do you use specific examples? Do you clearly explain their connections to your main point?)* You check on how clearly organized the paragraph is. *(Does it flow? Are ideas in the appropriate places? Do thoughts and/or details need to be added? Deleted? Rearranged?)*

It is also important to check your style. *(How are you using words? Are you varying sentence structure? Is your phrasing clear—to your reader?)*

One of the major elements to keep in mind as you revise is your *reading audience*. You are not just writing for yourself; you are writing for at least one other reader who does not necessarily share your background, experiences, and ways of thinking. It is important that you make your points clearly and coherently to your reader(s).

APPLICATION 8–2: Workshop Your Own Paragraph

Choose one of your own paragraphs and workshop it. Apply the peer-evaluation suggestions in this chapter.

_____

_____

_____

_____

_____

_____

_____

_____

_____

APPLICATION 8–3: Group-Workshopping Handout

Design a handout that you would use in group peer editing to help you evaluate and comment on each other's paragraphs. Here are some questions to get you started in designing this handout, but you don't have to limit yourself to answering just them:

■ What questions would you ask?

_____

_____

_____

■ What would you listen to and look for in your group members' drafts?

_____

_____

_____

_____

■ What would you look for in your own draft?

_____

_____

_____

_____

APPLICATION 8–4: One-on-One Peer-Evaluation Handout

Design a handout that you would use in one-on-one peer editing to help you evaluate and comment on your classmate's draft.

Here are some questions to help you get started:

■ What areas will you look at when you read the draft?

_____

_____

_____

_____

■ Do you want to write on the peer-evaluation sheet only or also on the draft?

_____

_____

_____

_____

■ What questions can you create to guide you as you read and comment?

_____

_____

_____

_____

■ What would you say to the writer once you're finished reading his/her draft?

_____

_____

_____

_____

■ What comments would you write in a letter to the writer?

_____

_____

_____

_____

APPLICATION 8–5: Group-Workshopping Styles/Activities

In all of the peer-evaluation contexts below, do the following:

■ Bring copies of your paragraph for everyone in your group.

■ Read your paragraph aloud while your group members listen.

■ Group members take notes on their copies of your paper.

■ You circle or put checks in the margins next to anything that makes you stumble or pause as you read.

Roundtable Reading

■ Each group member comments one at a time after the writer has read his/her paragraph aloud.

■ The writer then explains why he/she agrees or disagrees with each suggestion and what revisions he/she might make and why.

■ The group members return their copies to the writer.

Open Discussion

■ The group members point out strengths and areas needing revision, speaking in no particular order.

- The group members write notes on their copies of the writer's draft.
- The writer makes notes on his/her draft based on group members' suggestions.
- The group members return their copies of the writer's draft to the writer.

Facilitated Discussion

- The group must be small: five to ten people.
- The teacher is part of the group, takes notes, and asks for general impressions.
- The teacher only comments if the discussion gets off track, if the students share incorrect information, or if anyone has questions.
- When necessary, the teacher asks guiding questions to get the discussion started.

> - Roundtable reading and open-discussion workshop formats can also be done outside of class.
> - You can distribute copies of your writing to group members ahead of time so that they can read them and make notes/prepare comments before the workshop session.

Online Workshopping

For this type of evaluation, you need to be using a chat room or listserv space; your teacher will usually set one up for you.

- Each group member posts his/her first draft on the listserv.
- Group members post basic feedback (general comments on topic sentence, organization, content development, and grammar problems) on group members' drafts by a specific deadline.
- Each writer asks questions about any comments he/she doesn't understand or agree with. Then the writer posts a revision plan.
- Each writer revises and posts a second draft based on feedback.
- Group members now give specific, detailed feedback so that the writer can revise again.

Note: This type of peer evaluation can also work one-on-one.

APPLICATION 8–6: One-on-One Peer Evaluation

- Two writers exchange drafts in or out of class.

- Each writer writes comments on the other writer's draft.

- Each then writes an in-depth letter to the other, including detailed suggestions, questions, and general comments.

- Then the two meet face-to-face or online, return drafts with comments, and discuss their comments with each other.

CHAPTER **9**

Proofreading
The Final Step

To be a good writer, you not only have to write a great
deal but you have to care.
—*Anne Lamott*

PART 1: WHAT'S THE POINT?

Proofreading is the act of checking your writing very
carefully for errors in punctuation, spelling, formatting,
grammar, and vocabulary usage. It also involves identifying
and cleaning up typographical errors (typos). Proofreading
is the final step you need to take before submitting any of
your writing to another reader. It is essential to the quality
of your writing, yet many people ignore it because they are
unsure of what to look for.

Why should you proofread, anyway?

Credibility, embarrassment, professionalism, clarity, grades/quality ... the list goes on and on. These words are all basically about the professional appearance of your writing—and of *you* through your writing.

No matter how much time and effort you put into your writing, if it is unclear or full of errors, you will lose credibility with your readers, embarrassing yourself and decreasing your professional appearance. In addition, of course, anyone evaluating your work for a grade will award it a low grade for its low quality.

How do you proofread?

That is what this chapter will show you. Basically, proofreading is about finding and correcting all the sentence-level errors in your writing: typos; spelling, punctuation, and format errors; word choices; and any remaining grammatical errors. If you ignore this step, then your writing (and you) will look foolish.

PUNCTUATION

Punctuation, all those little marks and symbols used to help create meaning and clarity, is one area most of us have questions about. Punctuation does *not* exist just to drive you crazy! It is essential for making your words understandable to both yourself and your readers.

Here is an example to show how meaning can change with punctuation changes:

The Importance of Correct Punctuation[1]

(anonymous)

Dear John:

I want a man who knows what love is all about. You are generous, kind, thoughtful. People who are not like you admit to being useless and inferior. You have ruined me for other men. I yearn for you. I have no feelings whatsoever when we're apart. I can be forever happy—will you let me be yours?

Gloria

Dear John:

I want a man who knows what love is. All about you are generous, kind, thoughtful people, who are not like you. Admit to being useless and inferior. You have ruined me. For other men, I yearn. For you, I have no feelings whatsoever. When we're apart, I can be forever happy. Will you let me be?

Yours,
Gloria

Each of the above "Dear John" paragraphs has the same words in the same order, and yet each paragraph has a completely different meaning. In the first paragraph, Gloria obviously loves John and wants to keep him. In the second paragraph, Gloria obviously can't stand John and wants him to go away. How are these completely contrasting meanings possible when the words are exactly the same? *Punctuation.*

All the little marks (commas, semicolons, question marks, etc.) that separate words and phrases are punctuation marks. As you can see, they are absolutely essential for creating very specific meanings and messages. With a single period placement, you can change the entire message of your words. This is why punctuation is so important to writing.

Below is a series of common punctuation marks and their uses, with examples and explanations.

. PERIOD

A period is used to end sentences. (A period is called a "full stop" in British English, which some of you may have learned.) In most cases, two spaces go after a period that ends a sentence.

> Marriage demands patience and a great sense of humor.

> I wonder how I'll ever explain to my teacher that my cat really did bury my paper in the litter box.

➤ The previous sentence does not use a question mark because it isn't asking a direct question; rather, it is describing the writer's state of mind.

> Serial novels were common in early-twentieth- and late-nineteenth-century magazines.

➤ Notice, also, how a hyphen comes after "early" and "twentieth"; this is because the writer actually means "early-twentieth-century."

Periods are also used to mark abbreviations (shortened forms of words). For example, *et cetera* is commonly written as *etc.*

An important note: If an abbreviation also comes at the end of a sentence, use its period as the end period, too; don't add another period:

> The ranch needs more cattle, land, feed, etc.

A period can mark a one-word sentence, also:

> "Whatever." (*I am using quotation marks here only because it's dialogue.*)

➤   Sometimes, one word is set apart as a sentence, usually for emphasis or to create an effect. The one-word sentence above creates a sarcastic tone.

, COMMA

Commas are used to set off phrases that interrupt the flow of a sentence but add important information:

> My aunt, whom I love very much, is moving closer to my brothers and me.

A comma is used with coordinating conjunctions (for, and, nor, but, or, yet, so—FANBOYS) to join two sentences. This can be the toughest one to figure out at first, but it gets clear with practice. A comma goes *before* a conjunction that joins two **clauses** because the writer needs to transition from one clause to the next:

> The net has a hole in it, so the trout got away when Jim tried to scoop it out of the water.

> He wasn't arrested, but the highway patrol will be keeping an eye on his driving for a few weeks.

> Note: The word "clause" simply means a group of words. An **independent clause** can stand alone as a sentence; a **dependent clause** needs to be attached to another clause in order to complete an idea.

Commas usually are used to set off introductory (dependent) clauses when they have four or more words (e.g., look for "when," "although," and "since" at the beginning of sentences).

An introductory clause signals *only* the beginning of an idea; you have to complete your thought. The comma clears up any confusion about what goes with what, too. Here are some examples:

> Although it was pouring rain, Dave ran outside in his boxers.

> When the horse broke loose from the corral, she left a trail of broken wood behind her.

> Instead of yelling at all the drivers to hurry up, leave earlier so that you're not in such a hurry.

Commas are also used to mark three or more items in a series. The reason commas are not needed for just two items is because the word "and" is used to join the two items together. Also, some items are more than one word long, so be sure you know what goes with what before inserting commas:

> I drove to the mall, shopped at Banana Republic, and ate a lousy lunch of tasteless tacos and warm cola.

Addresses

A comma is placed between the name of a city and the state it is in:

> Bensonville, AK *(Note the two capital letters used for state abbreviations.)*

If you're writing a city and state in a sentence, then you also put a comma after the state (unless the state is the last word in the sentence, in which case you put a period after it):

> I went to Bensonville, Arkansas, for my birthday.

Dates

When a date is written as month-day-year, a comma follows the day of the month:

> January 20, 2001

If you're writing a date in a sentence, then you also put a comma after the year (unless the year ends the sentence, in which case you put a period after it):

> Our flight on January 20, 2001, was nonstop.

No commas are used between just the month and year:

> January 2001

No commas are used when the day comes first:

> 20 January 2001

; SEMICOLON

Semicolons are great for creating sentence variety (so that every sentence doesn't flow and sound the same, which can put your readers to sleep).

A semicolon is used to join two *independent clauses* (complete sentences):

Still shots catch the general nature scenes; action shots catch the unexpected movements and creatures within those nature scenes.

A semicolon is sometimes used with transitional words.

➤ (Notice below that a comma follows a transitional word that begins a new clause.)

Transitional words help readers move from one clause to another. Here are some examples:

Consequently	However	Indeed
Otherwise	Therefore	

I played basketball in high school; however, I switched to baseball in college.

I know the recipe; indeed, I have made albondigas soup for years, and my family loves it.

If you just crammed the two parts of the sentence together without a strong enough stopping marker, then your readers would get confused trying to figure out where one idea ended and another one began:

Incorrect: I know the recipe I have made albondigas soup for years my family loves it.

Below is a passage that has no punctuation or formatting. Even if you get the main idea quickly, think about the effort it takes to figure out where phrases and sentences end and begin. Now think about what your reader would do if this were your paragraph; he or she would quit reading and go on to something else.

as with all electrical fixture work replacement and repair instructions should be followed carefully use common sense when preparing your work area to avoid obvious dangers such as water sharp objects inadequate tools or rickety support structures take extra care when working with electricity being sure to ground your body and turn the electricity off at the correct fuse before beginning work keep all children and pets away from the area to avoid electrocution or other injury

How hard was it for you to understand each sentence of this paragraph? Semicolons are used to mark lengthy items that already use commas within a series:

She was hot, tired, but happy; eager to end the hike; proud that she'd made it fifteen miles.

: COLON

Colons are used to set off lists or defining points after statements—a big help in avoiding repetitiveness:

What he wanted was a bunch of materials: tubes, copper wire, duct tape, and sealing wax.

If you didn't use a colon, you'd create an unnecessarily repetitive sentence:

Repetitive: What he wanted was a bunch of materials. He wanted tubes, copper wire, duct tape, and sealing wax.

Here is another example:

I want the following supplies delivered by Wednesday: flour, peanuts, beef jerky, chocolate, chicken soup, and multivitamins.

Colons can be used to divide two independent clauses when the second clause explains the first clause:

Driving on good shock absorbers is like riding a horse at full gallop: you get a smooth ride at high speeds.

Colons are also used for times:

12:00 p.m.

They are used to show ratios:

1:4 (one to four)

And colons are used before subtitles:

Mary Matthews: The Life of a Nature Photographer Who Wrestled with Bears

' APOSTROPHE

Apostrophes are *not* used to form plurals—know your plural vs. possessive forms (e.g., countries vs. country's)

Apostrophes are used to show possession—"of" (if you can form the construction "of so and so," then you usually have a possessive):

> This is Josefa's Honda. (the Honda of Josefa)
>
> Rick's keyboard was missing from the computer shipment. (the keyboard of Rick)

When one item is owned by two people, you only use an apostrophe for the second person:

> Joey and Mike's bicycle. (bicycle of Joey and Mike)

However, when a different item is owned by each person, you use an apostrophe for each owner:

> Joey's and Mike's bicycles. (bicycle of Joey and bicycle of Mike)

? QUESTION MARK

Question marks are used to indicate a question being asked:

> He wants it today? Today!?
>
> Is this statement true? How do you know?
>
> Why? *(a one-word question)*

However, writing that you "wonder" about something is a statement not a question, so you do not use a question mark:

> I wonder how often my irises will bloom before I have to replace the bulbs.

" " QUOTATION MARKS

Quotation marks are sometimes used to set off words or phrases in a sentence:

> She saw the word "paisley" written on the instructions, but she didn't know what it meant.

Quotation marks are also used to set off dialogue:

> "Marcy," he asked, "How do I replace the cartridge?"

➤ Notice the placement of the comma and question mark inside the quotation marks in the above sentence. Question marks don't always go inside quotation marks (although commas and periods *always* go inside closing quotation marks), but in this case the question is the actual dialogue.

"Well, you finally made it. We were wondering if you got lost," said Ron.

Quotation marks can also create emphasis or irony:

I was so "happy" to see the lizard on my doorstep.

They also set off quotations from outside sources:

According to Ramsey, "Heat is produced from the friction of two elephants rubbing their trunks together" (78).

➤ The above sentence shows MLA documentation style; APA would look like this: (p. 78).

Quotation marks are also used for titles of short works: articles, all poems except book-length poems, book chapters, short stories, unpublished speeches, essays, song titles, and TV episodes.

An episode is one of the weekly or daily versions of a running show.

[] PARENTHESES

Parentheses are used to set off important information that otherwise would interrupt the flow of a sentence. *Always read what is in them!*

Pick up a copy of the novel (located at Shay's Bookstore) for class next week.

➤ In the above sentence, the location is important because you need to know where to get the book, but it also interrupts the main point of the sentence.

Spelling note: Parenthesis vs. -ses (singular vs. plural). The plural forms of words ending in -sis are spelled using -ses.

- HYPHEN

Hyphens are used to create compound words (words created from more than one word), especially compound adjectives.

A compound adjective is formed when two or more adjectives come before what they are describing:

The twenty-year-old man. ("Twenty-year-old" is a compound adjective.)

If the adjectives followed what they described, they would not be hyphenated:

The man is twenty years old.

Hyphens are also used to form dashes (--).
Hyphens also connect some prefixes to some words:

non-native (*Non* is the prefix.)

Hyphens used to be used commonly to separate words that ran over onto the next lines; however, this sort of use is no longer encouraged. Instead, you should write the entire word on the next line rather than separating it.

-- DASH

Dashes are formed using two hyphens, with no spaces between the hyphens or on either side of them.

> In most of this guide, the two hyphens in a dash are shown as a single line; this is a common practice in books. Also note that some word-processing programs will convert the two hyphens in a dash to one line, which is fine.

Dashes set off important information that otherwise would interrupt the flow of a sentence:

Still shots catch general nature scenes--sunsets, ocean vistas, mountain views, ranches--that we often pass by too quickly to notice.

A dash can be used with a fragment to create emphasis:

My dog Pogo is curled up in his bed, snoring, paws hanging out--what a life.

Sometimes dashes are used to set off dialogue:

--What? Where did you see this?
--Sam's place. We were out back, and the flash almost blinded us.

Dashes can also be used to indicate interruptions, something left unspoken:

"I said I don't want--" *(I am using quotation marks here only because it's dialogue.)*

❗ EXCLAMATION MARK

Exclamation marks show emphasis:

She's amazing!

They are used to show direct orders:

Do it now!

Go to your room!

Catch the goat!

Exclamation marks are also used to indicate anger, surprise, and other intense emotions in dialogue:

"No, dang it! I didn't mean what she thought I meant."

"I thought we were going to the movies tonight!"

TYPOS AND OMISSIONS

Typo is short for **typographical error**—any error in formatting or writing, usually adding in or leaving out what you don't want, like an extra space or letter(s), or extra words:

Get th ball.

How, do you do this?

OTHER GRAMMATICAL ISSUES

Singular and Plural Forms   *Verbs*–Usually, verbs in English do not use an *s* for the plural form; they use *s* for the singular form. This is the exact opposite of what many people think it should be logically:

He drives an old El Camino.

They drive an old El Camino.

Neither Martha nor Lon drives an old El Camino.

➤   "Neither ... nor" creates a singular subject in the above sentence; see the "either/or" examples given on page 123.

>   Both Martha and Lon drive old El Caminos.

In the above sentence, "and" creates a plural subject; see the discussion of compound subjects on page 123.

Nouns–Usually nouns in English use an *s* for plural forms:

>   dogs
>
>   soccer balls *(the adjective "soccer" describes the ball but does not have an "s")*
>
>   Martians (A group of Martians landed on the football field outside of town.)

Some nouns, however, do not use *s* because they are already plural in meaning:

>   people
>
>   children

Words that have -*st* endings still need an extra *s* when they are plural:

>   scientists

Some word endings change when the word goes from singular to plural:

>   country *(singular)*   countries *(plural)*

Adjectives–Adjectives (words that describe) in English do not use *s* for plural:

>   crimson roses
>
>   rusty cans
>
>   A group of grumpy grandpas raided the discount store down the street.

Words like "many" and "much" can sometimes create confusion, but you'll get used to them.
"Many" refers to individual items:

>   Many trucks roared down the entrance ramp.

"Much" refers to an amount that can't be individually counted:

>   We are not expecting much bad weather this month.

"Many" would be used to refer to individual storms:

We are not expecting many storms this month.

Subject-Verb Agreement Subjects and verbs have to agree, which means that plural subjects use plural verbs and singular subjects use singular verbs.

It is not always easy to use correct agreement. Here are some tips to help you with challenging agreement formations:

INTERVENING PREPOSITIONAL PHRASES

The group of old buildings was preserved by the historical society.

➤ Here, "of old buildings" is just a prepositional phrase that describes the subject, which is "group." "Group" is a singular word, so the verb "was" has to be singular.

EITHER/OR CONSTRUCTIONS

Either Sara or the Pattens were in charge of the community barbecue.

Either the Pattens or Sara was in charge of the community barbecue.

➤ In an either/or construction, the subject nearest to the verb determines whether it is plural or singular.

COMPOUND SUBJECTS

The Pattens and Sara were in charge of the community barbecue.

➤ Here, the subject is a combination of the Pattens and Sara joined by "and." This is called a *compound subject*, and compound subjects are always plural.

Pronunciation

Vowels (*a, e, i, o, u*) have what are called **long** and **short sounds**:

A: at, small (short *a*), aim (long *a*)

E: every (short *e*), even (first *e* is long; second *e* is short)

I: into (short *i*), I (long *i*)

O: on, of (short *o*), only (long *o*)

U: unusual (first *u* is short; second two are long), user (long *u*)

Vowel sounds are sometimes determined by how many of the same consonant are in the middle of a word. A single consonant may indicate a long vowel sound, a double consonant a short sound:

dining (eating), not dinning (a "din" is a loud racket)

Some vowel constructions change sound depending on what words they are used in, *ough*, for instance:

> bough (ow), cough (off), through (oo), enough (uff), ought (awt), thorough (oh)

All of these changing pronunciations demonstrate why it's so important to read *and* write, not just to do one or the other. You can look up pronunciations in a **dictionary**. And you can practice them when you speak.

Idioms/Idiomatic Expressions   Idioms are figurative phrases that cannot be translated literally, and they can confuse many people, particularly ESL writers.

A sentence like, "He's a bull in a china shop" makes no sense when translated literally. "A bull in a china shop" means someone who is very clumsy; you don't want that person around your breakable glassware. But if you do not know the figurative (nonliteral) meaning of the expression, then you will simply be confused by it. Below, I have listed three web sites about idiomatic expressions and other ESL issues. These web sites are also helpful to native English speakers. They will lead you to other good web sites, as well:

> *Aardvark's English Forum and EFL Resources.*
> http://www.english-forum.com/.

> Dave Sperling and Dennis Oliver. *ESL Idiom Page.*
> http://www.pacificnet.net/~sperling/idioms.cgi.

> *VLC Hong Kong Virtual Language Center 2001.*
> http://vlc.polyu.edu.hk/.

Prepositions   Prepositions show relationships between words. They often become a problem for writers because they are not easy to define. For example, how do you define "on"? Prepositions create relationships between parts of a sentence, usually between the subject and its object.

Tip: To understand *which* prepositions go *where*, you have to read as much as you can and see the words in action. This is a prime example of how reading and writing work together.

Here are some examples:

> The book *[subject]* lies **on** *[preposition]* the table *[object of the preposition]*.

I *[subject]* am sitting between *[preposition]* two cats *[objects of the preposition]*.

The pickup truck careened under *[preposition]* the bridge *[object of the preposition]* and hurtled through *[preposition]* the tunnel *[object of the preposition]* at eighty miles an hour.

Prepositions show relationships:

over, above

on

in, inside

under, beneath

Some Prepositions

About	Above	Against	Among
Around	At	Before	Behind
Below	Beneath	Beside(s)	Between
By	Despite	Down	During
From	In	Inside	Near
Next to	Of	Off	On
Onto	Out	Outside	Over
Past	Since	Through(out)	To
Toward	Under	Underneath	Until
Up	Upon	Within	Without

Definite and Indefinite Articles   Some of you have first languages that do not use **definite** ("the") and **indefinite** ("a," "an") **articles**. Therefore, when writing in English, you may be uncertain about when and how to use "a," "an," and "the." Identifying when to use "a," "an," and "the" also can be a problem for native English speakers.

Here are some rules for using definite and indefinite articles:

"The" is used when you are referring to something specific:

the sky,   the clouds,   the three gophers.

However, "the" is not usually necessary when you are referring to a general situation or condition:

> *Illness* is common at this time of year.

➤ Does the following sentence confuse you with its use of "the"?

> The flu is constant in December, but colds are just as frequent.

➤ Are you wondering why there is no "the" before "colds"? In this case, "colds" designates a general condition, whereas "the flu" designates a specific illness.

When is "a" or "an" used? An indefinite article is used when referring to one of a type:

> I have *a* headache.
>
> I am interested in *a* store that sells ties.
>
> I would like *an* answer to my question, please.

When using "a" or "an," remember that "an" comes before a vowel sound to help the speaker's tongue transition from one sound to the next: an apple, an orange, an orangutan, an interesting opportunity, an hour (because the *h* is silent). It would be awkward in English pronunciation to say "a apple," or "a orange," even though people sometimes do this when speaking.

On the other hand, "a" comes before a consonant sound: a grape, a marvelous time, a general, a flea market, a retro style, a unique outfit (because the *u* sounds like *y*). Again, this is to help the mouth move between words more smoothly.

> Ricky has the *[a specific condition]* flu, but he got a *[a general shot]* vitamin shot yesterday. An *["n" before "a" in "ancient," one doctor, but not yet one we know]* ancient doctor gave the shot to him, and Ricky's mom was nervous at first. But the *[now we know that it's the specific doctor who gave Ricky the specific shot]* doctor knew what she was doing and stuck the *[the specific needle for the shot that Ricky was given]* needle as gently as possible where it needed to go. Ricky's mom got him a *[just a general toy car at this point]* toy car afterward; he was crying so loudly she could barely hear herself think. But she told him he was a *[general description of brave-boy behavior]* brave boy and would feel a *[part of the word phrase "a lot"]* lot better soon. In a *[a general time increment]* half hour, he was grinning from ear to ear as he played with the *[now we know it's the particular car his mom got him]* car; he had completely forgotten about the *[the specific doctor Ricky went to]* doctor and the *[the actual shot he was given]* shot.

SPELLING

S on Word Endings   Remember to put *s* on the ends of words like "scientist" when you are forming the plural: "scientists," "activists," "naturalists," capitalists," etc.

"I before E"   An old saying begins, "*I* before *e*, except after *c*" (e.g., "receive," "conceive"). It continues like this: "and when sounding like *a* as in 'neighbor' and 'weigh.'" This can be a helpful memory device for you. Once in a while, you will find a word that does not fit the rules, like "weird." Don't let that make you nervous: you will learn the correct spelling over time.

Single and Double Consonants   Once you know the pronunciation of some words, it is easier to figure out whether they need single or double consonants. A long vowel sound can indicate that a word is spelled with a single consonant; a short sound may suggest a double consonant. For example, if you know that "dining" has a long *i* sound, you will know to use only one *n* in the middle. Or, if you know that "thinning" has a short *i* sound, you know to use two *n*'s: "His hair was thinning."

Commonly Misspelled Words (Common Homonyms)   Many words are easily misspelled simply because you might not know what they look like, only what they sound like. **Homonyms** are words that sound alike but are spelled differently (e.g., "there," "their," and "they're"). You will learn these differences with time and practice. Here are some examples:

a lot = many

allot = to portion out

(There is no "alot")

accept = to allow, approve

except = to exclude, leave out

conscience = a sense of right and wrong

conscious = aware

knew = had information about

new = just created, not old

through = a preposition related to movement (I ran through the house.)

threw = an action (I threw the ball.)

loose = not tight

lose = unable to find

choose = present tense form of "to choose"

chose = past tense form of "to choose"

then = used for sequential events (Then the doorbell rang.)

than = used to make comparisons (I am older than you.)

effect = usually a noun, the result of something (My soggy lawn was the effect of four days of rain.)

affect = usually a verb, to influence or pretend (Her argument affected the group's decision.)

write = the act of putting words on paper

right = correct; the opposite of "left"

aloud = spoken

allowed = approved, given permission for

Using Spell-Check   Do not rely only on spell-check programs to catch everything; they will not identify when you have used the wrong word but spelled it correctly (e.g., if you use "form" where you wanted to write "from").

PART 2: APPLICATIONS

The following activities and exercises will give you experience in proofreading on a sentence level and working directly with punctuation.

APPLICATION 9–1: Proofreading Questions to Ask Yourself

What questions do you need to ask yourself before and during proofreading? List them here:

_____

_____

_____

_____

_____

_____

_____

_____

_____

_____

APPLICATION 9–2: Punctuation 1

Below are series of sentences categorized under various punctuation marks. For each set of sentences, make the appropriate corrections.

Comma   Place commas where they are needed in each of the sentences below. If you feel a comma is not necessary, then leave it out and explain why. Refer to the section in this chapter on commas to help you.

SET 1

1. Films like *Titanic* and *Pearl Harbor* both of them blockbusters attempt to retell history.

_____

_____

2. Although I had a fever yesterday I feel healthy now.

_____

_____

3. Finally the concert's over but the audience is yelling for an encore.

_____

_____

4. Loaded with fish bananas and hay bales the truck drove off to the next town.

_____

_____

5. My plans are to drive to Palmer Wyoming and settle down on seventy-six acres.

_____

_____

6. Regardless of the holidays you celebrate your family probably has some great recipes for holiday meals.

_____

_____

7. After growing up with three sets of foster parents Maggie wanted to make sure her children had lots of stability.

_____

_____

8. Marta crafts gorgeous lampshades from handmade paper and she makes the paper herself too.

_____

_____

9. Serious studying can be done in two ways but at the moment I don't care.

_____

_____

10. Three houses on our block went without electricity for forty-eight hours so the inhabitants had to stay in motels.

_____

_____

1. Sal's muffin recipe calls for blueberries blackberries strawberries and orange rind.

_____

_____

2. Something must be done about the leak in the swimming pool but first we need to get the money for the repairs.

_____

_____

3. Sheila was angry for Tamela was forty-five minutes late.

_____

_____

4. Do you want lemon or do you want lime?

_____

_____

5. I'm either going home this weekend or I'm going to look for the nearest motel room so I can get away from my roommates.

_____

_____

6. Seventeen flavors are listed yet she just wants chocolate.

_____

_____

7. Are Greg's dogs border collies Australian shepherds or pit bulls?

_____

_____

8. Sharon is not picky about the vegetables she eats nor does she like them all.

9. Second take a left at the oak tree even though there is no street sign.

10. Save the turkey breast for me but give the drumsticks to Josh.

Semicolon

Semicolon   Place semicolons where they are needed in each of the sentences below. If you feel a semicolon is not necessary, then leave it out and explain why. Refer to the section in this chapter on semicolons to help you.

SET 1

1. Our favorite dogs are pit bulls they are gentle and intelligent when treated well.

2. Dan's computer had a breakdown it chewed up a disk then crashed the hard drive.

3. My major is nursing however, I'm thinking of adding a minor in psychology.

4. Carla crammed a tent, sleeping bag, and kerosene stove into the back of the truck called Mike on her cell phone, reminding him to check the dogs and drove off to Canyonlands.

5. Changing the spark plugs should be an easy task I stripped the threads on one, however.

_____

_____

6. I've heard of two film versions of *The Corn Is Green* my favorite is the one starring Katherine Hepburn.

_____

_____

7. Poodles are supposed to be one of the most intelligent dogs however, they are often represented as stupid and yappy.

_____

_____

8. Sam and LeeAnne used to work on cars now they need special training to repair newer, computerized vehicles.

_____

_____

9. I can smell Mario's simmering pasta fasul it's making me crazy to wait for the thick soup because I'm starved.

_____

_____

10. Sal grew up with cats and dogs consequently, he loves both equally.

_____

_____

SET 2

1. After searching for ten minutes, I found Kurt in the backyard, surrounded with lawn mower parts he was looking for an oil leak.

_____

_____

2. I finished putting the grill together in two hours unfortunately, three pieces were still mysteriously unaccounted for.

   _____

   _____

3. Finally, the plane landed I was really stiff after sitting for eight hours.

   _____

   _____

4. Stereo speakers have changed in size over the past three decades now you can get a huge sound from a tiny package.

   _____

   _____

5. A sparrow landed on the picnic table she studied me as I ate my sandwich (probably hoping for crumbs).

   _____

   _____

6. A good catch isn't the only thing Serge looks for on his fishing trips he wants peace and quiet most of all.

   _____

   _____

7. The movie was too long although I like character development, it could have been accomplished in two hours instead of three.

   _____

   _____

8. All Mimi wanted was a nap she had to drop her kids off at soccer practice first, though.

   _____

   _____

9. Right now a quilt just hangs over my living room window eventually, I want to use pieces of the quilt and other fabrics to create more attractive window coverings.

   _____

   _____

10. Phil walked into the store to get a CD burner he left with a new computer.

_____

_____

Colon   Each sentence below needs at least one colon. Insert a colon where you think it is necessary and explain why you placed it there. Refer to the section in this chapter on colons to help you.

SET 1

1. Paint what you see shadows, colors, tints, and shapes.

_____

_____

2. Class meets in the museum lobby at 100 P.M.

_____

_____

3. No bets can be filed the horses have left the starting gate.

_____

_____

4. Jake's serenity was short-lived for the following reason his four kids got home and demanded that he play basketball with them.

_____

_____

5. He's familiar with the recipe a spicy blend of pepper, garlic, and scallops.

_____

_____

6. Serious studying can be done in two ways cramming intensely the night before an exam or taking notes and doing readings as they're assigned so you can just review your notes quickly the night before the exam.

_____

_____

7. Marta crafts gorgeous handmade paper from a variety of ingredients mulberry and banana fibers and paper egg cartons.

_____

_____

8. Helene took her gift certificate to the kitchen store and picked up several long-awaited appliances a large food processor, a bread machine, and a meat grinder.

_____

_____

9. Rick ordered an assortment of mushrooms straws, morels, and portabellas.

_____

_____

10. Three houses on our block went without electricity for forty-eight hours the DiVideos', the Mullers', and the Greens'.

_____

_____

SET 2

1. Several scuba divers reported the same findings a neon-blue fish that, as far as they knew, hadn't been discovered before.

_____

_____

2. We want the following supplies for our classroom one white board, one chalkboard, colored chalk and white-board markers, and a large pad of newsprint.

_____

_____

3. The cake wouldn't rise, and we realized an essential ingredient was missing baking powder.

_____

_____

4. The painter of this farm scene is trying to convey a message the illusion of rural tranquility.

_____

_____

5. You never know what situations you might face when growing roses aphids, mildew, spider mites—or gorgeous, healthy plants full of huge blooms and deep green leaves.

_____

_____

6. I was stuck because I wanted both vehicles a small gas-saver and a straight-six four-wheel-drive.

_____

_____

7. My friends and I cook up a fun blend of recipes for Thanksgiving turkey with sausage stuffing, meat and chicken tamales, and an array of side dishes that boggle the imagination.

_____

_____

8. I can never get it straight either the timer goes off when the dough is ready to go into the oven or when it is ready to be kneaded again.

_____

_____

9. Save it for later 7 00 P.M. or 8 00 P.M.

_____

_____

10. The carpet has all the right fluorescent colors orange, pink, and purple.

_____

_____

Apostrophe   Each sentence below needs at least one apostrophe. Insert apostrophes where you think they are necessary (if they are necessary) and explain why you placed them there. Refer to the section in this chapter on apostrophes to help you.

SET 1

1. Many countries wilderness areas are growing instead of shrinking.

_____

_____

2. Many companies advertise for jobs they dont intend to fill.

_____

_____

3. Jessicas and Karens houses were designed by the same firm of architects.

_____

_____

4. Theyre coming, and Im not ready.

_____

_____

5. This poems purpose is to convince people that all dreams are about being hungry.

_____

_____

6. Is that Jaimes car parked out front?

_____

_____

7. So where is the postal worker with todays mail?

_____

_____

8. All the flowers petals were still fresh after six hours.

_____

_____

9. Are Troys and Hughs bikes in good enough condition for a road trip?

_____

_____

10. I cant find descriptions of the countrys political system.

_____

_____

SET 2

1. Mark and Beckis house was the first in the neighborhood to sell for over one hundred thousand dollars.

_____

_____

2. The teddy bears paws were coming unraveled.

_____

_____

3. How did Janes lifestyle get to be so complex?

_____

_____

4. With his voice, Joes singing career is going to take off.

_____

_____

5. Their bodies requirements are all different.

_____

_____

6. Poodles intelligence is very high, but they are often represented as stupid and yappy.

_____

_____

7. Finally, the airports control tower came into view from the coach section; we landed five minutes later.

_____

_____

8. Each bands musical style is different, but I like them all.

_____

_____

9. Mikes cigarettes lay on the kitchen counter, but he was nowhere in sight.

_____

_____

10. The house is only four years old; however, its paint is already flaking.

_____

_____

Question Mark   Insert question marks where you feel they are necessary within or following the sentences below. If you decide that a question mark is not necessary at the end of a particular sentence, then leave it out, insert the correct punctuation mark, and explain your decision. Refer to the section in this chapter on question marks to help you.

SET 1

1. How can this be

   _____

   _____

2. You fixed the brakes, didn't you

   _____

   _____

3. He asked if I was hungry

   _____

   _____

4. Maggie asked, "Are you okay"

   _____

   _____

5. Stan questioned whether the script was really ready to go into production

   _____

   _____

6. Is concrete sand and cement, or is cement sand and concrete

   _____

   _____

7. How can I be creative when there's a vacuum cleaner blasting away in the same room

   _____

   _____

8. You wanted it decaf, right

   _____

   _____

9. Does Nick want to come to the movie with the rest of us

_____

_____

10. How about the Jacksons

_____

_____

SET 2

1. Have we really discovered all the planets in the solar system

_____

_____

2. What holiday recipes does your family make

_____

_____

3. Joe asked, "Are they at the party"

_____

_____

4. I wonder how many people have completed the twenty-mile hike in one day

_____

_____

5. I wondered, "How many people have completed that hike in one day"

_____

_____

6. If Desi parked her car on 10th Street, why are we looking for it on 11th Street

_____

_____

7. How many cabbages will fit in a five-quart stockpot

_____

_____

8. So you call yourself a river rat: What's that

_____

_____

9. Are you aware of all the situations you will have to deal with

_____

_____

10. How can I be a better parent to my kids and a better daughter to my parents

_____

_____

Quotation Marks   Place quotation marks where you think they belong in the following sentences. Refer to the section in this chapter on quotation marks to help you.

SET 1

1. Don't forget the milk, Mom yelled as we ran out the back door.

_____

_____

2. Sam asked Chris, Are you going to the game tonight?

_____

_____

3. Terry, how do I replace the water filter yelled Mark.

_____

_____

4. Yeah, Shelly was thrilled to find out that her sister had totaled the car.

_____

_____

5. As stated by Beckman, If you drop a fire truck and a feather from the Empire State Building, they will both hit the ground at the same time (39). I don't believe it.

_____

_____

6. Saintly sure isn't the first word I'd think of when trying to describe my close friends.

7. Are the pies ready to come out of the oven yet? Arlene asked.

8. And it's a strong finish for number fourteen, the commentator yelled.

9. The term spirituality takes a lot of time to write about with insight.

10. Pam wrote a poem entitled Six Bonnets for Charlie, and none of us could figure out what it meant.

SET 2

1. Max, she yelled, where are you?

2. Six rounds of poker, and you don't play cards? Yikes! You'll have a great time, she said to Frances.

3. The circus has an act I want to see: Wanda and Her Amazing Penguins.

4. Percy Shelley's Ode on a Grecian Urn is a famous early-nineteenth-century poem.

5. All I heard was, Meow, when I opened the front door; my hungry cat was insisting that she hadn't been fed in a hundred years.

_____

_____

6. As I headed out the door, Mary yelled, Don't forget the grocery list!

_____

_____

7. Kim published her essay, The Setting Sun, in a well-known nature magazine.

_____

_____

8. The point, she said, is to make sure to set a strong seal around the skylights to avoid leaks.

_____

_____

9. I always read the Gardening Tips section first when I get my garden magazine.

_____

_____

10. My favorite _I Love Lucy_ episode is Lucy Raises Chickens.

_____

_____

Parentheses   Insert parentheses where needed in the sentences below. Explain why you use or do not use them in each sentence. Refer to the section in this chapter on parentheses to help you.

SET 1

1. She found it in the back room a dismal hole if ever there was one.

_____

_____

2. Jameson argues that "wheels were invented at least 10,000 years ago" 141.

_____

_____

3. Jill blew out a tire in one of the many potholes which should have been filled in months ago on Springer Street.

_____

_____

4. The Childes Mansion a museum now used to be the center of this town's political activity.

_____

_____

5. Five times last month an unusually high number, Dorothy's shepherd jumped the six-foot wall in the backyard.

_____

_____

6. Santa Claus a favorite Christmas figure is depicted in an enormous variety of costumes.

_____

_____

7. I won a six-day Caribbean cruise I sure needed it, which I took for my birthday.

_____

_____

8. Parrots apart from the feathers and squawking make fun pets.

_____

_____

9. Potato chips my favorite snack food are on sale at the grocery store this week.

_____

_____

10. After dinner the waiter brought by a tray full of desserts not that we had room for them, which looked too beautiful to eat.

_____

_____

SET 2

1. The centuries-old gothic cathedrals in Europe tributes to the incredible artistry of stained-glass artists, stone masons, and architects will still be standing five hundred years from now.

_____

_____

2. When Frank and Liza moved into their first home a little two-bedroom split-level, they painted each room a different color.

_____

_____

3. My eight-year-old car except for the carburetor, which I have to replace still runs so well that I'll probably keep it for another eight years.

_____

_____

4. The cactus garden not as thorny as I thought it would be was in full bloom when I went to visit it.

_____

_____

5. My binoculars not particularly powerful didn't help me see much at the concert.

_____

_____

6. Manny's collection of art prints all examples of cubism is now worth thousands of dollars.

_____

_____

7. Jerry has created ceramic vases and dishware an art I've never mastered for more than fifteen years.

_____

_____

8. I had to tell Tom that the computer he'd ordered was out of stock which was unfortunate since he was using mine too much.

_____

_____

9. Lea can't build snowmen snowpeople? in Hawaii.

_____

_____

10. Common human emotions love, anger, excitement, fear often surface unexpectedly.

_____

_____

Dashes   The following fifteen sentences need at least one dash. Decide where to place the dash in each case, and then explain why you put it where you did.

1. Trinh watered the garden a complicated task since it covered two acres.

_____

_____

2. Charging through the store a bull in a china shop Seth knocked over two cabinets before slowing down.

_____

_____

3. He was a man with a mission not that he knew what that mission was.

_____

_____

4. Darry started to talk: "Well, I'm on my w"

_____

_____

5. Hideous that's how they described the flavor.

_____

_____

6. Stephanie's dress satiny and close-fitting was a sensation with the guys.

_____

_____

7. My camera strap broke as I peered over the edge of the cliff what an expensive accident!

8. Simple that's how she described the tiling process anyway.

9. Our balloon ride over the city awesome camera shots included cost a bundle.

10. Sit on it to hold the lid down the only way to close a full suitcase.

11. Barbarita finished her sentence a miracle considering how many times Beth interrupted her.

12. Peaceful maybe refreshing definitely: I looked forward to the swim.

13. Remaining centered on the beam, she leaped into three back flips quite a feat for a ten-year-old gymnast.

14. Watchful that's the term Mick used to describe her neighbor.

15. I hauled, dumped, and raked several wheelbarrow loads of gravel today never again!

Hyphens   The following fifteen sentences need at least one hyphen. Decide where to place the hyphen in each case and then explain why you put it where you did.

1. How can you expect so much from a three year old?

   _____

   _____

2. We weren't prepared for a seventeen mile hike (mostly uphill).

   _____

   _____

3. While late twentieth and early twenty first century music styles didn't seem too different to Jake, they seemed wildly different to Monique.

   _____

   _____

4. How can we get Monica to bring her twelve year old daughter to the party?

   _____

   _____

5. Carl's holier than thou attitude kept a lot of people from taking him seriously.

   _____

   _____

6. Those fake friendly people are just a group of wanna be's, so I ignore them.

   _____

   _____

7. "Meals by candlelight": that's what the so called fancy restaurant advertised on a badly painted sign.

   _____

   _____

8. All the fancy scrollwork gave the church a gingerbread house appearance at first glance.

   _____

   _____

9. We need a four wheel drive for those rugged mountain roads.

_____

_____

10. Jake can be extremely self absorbed when he's under a lot of stress.

_____

_____

11. Hall's specialty was mid to late seventeenth century politics in the United States.

_____

_____

12. Chuy has worked for fifteen years with white hot metal and has a lot of scars to prove it.

_____

_____

13. The Millers and Johnsons have a thirty year history of fighting, but even those who were there at the time can't remember what started it all.

_____

_____

14. We live in Alaska; are the trees extreme cold hardy?

_____

_____

15. Well, Dave seemed mild mannered, until he didn't get his way.

_____

_____

Variety   The following sentences need a variety of punctuation marks. Decide which punctuation marks are the most appropriate for each sentence, insert the correct marks, and explain your decisions.

1. The term blowhard means someone who uses a lot of words to say very little

_____

_____

2. How can Ted pay for three tickets if he only has money for two

_____

_____

3. Skiing has given me these injuries two concussions, a broken ankle, and three sprained wrists

_____

_____

4. Edgar Allan Poes poem The Raven has been adapted for at least two films one starring Bela Lugosi and the other starring Vincent Price and Boris Karloff

_____

_____

5. When Mariana fell asleep the stove exploded

_____

_____

6. Chris is adamant Madisonville is over the next hill

_____

_____

7. Simplify your choices pay attention to your budget and make decisions that will give you peace of mind

_____

_____

8. The band practiced for hours therefore they were ready to blow the audience away with their new sound and pounding rhythms

_____

_____

9. Emad who writes restaurant reviews for the *Gazette* got food poisoning last night

_____

_____

10. First get the money and stop at the bank

_____

_____

11. Sarahs pen glows in the dark but thats nothing like Martas fluorescent shoes

_____

_____

12. I wonder what Lisa and Kate are doing in Tahiti

_____

_____

13. Tim and Mikes truck got four flats while they were four wheeling

_____

_____

14. The college application is due December 29 2005

_____

_____

APPLICATION 9–3: Punctuation 2

Re-read the two "Dear John" letters earlier in this chapter. Explain how punctuation marks change and create meaning in the two versions. Give specific examples. Explain what each punctuation mark is, what it does, and the meaning it creates.

First version:

_____

_____

_____

_____

_____

_____

_____

_____

_____

Second version:

_____

_____

_____

_____

_____

_____

_____

_____

Choose sentences from your own writing, identify the punctuation marks you used, and explain why you used them. Decide also whether you are using punctuation marks correctly.

First sentence:

_____

_____

_____

_____

_____

_____

_____

_____

_____

Second sentence:

_____

_____

_____

_____

_____

_____

_____

_____

_____

Third sentence:

_____

_____

_____

_____

_____

_____

_____

_____

Fourth sentence:

_____

_____

_____

_____

_____

_____

_____

_____

_____

_____

Fifth sentence:

_____

_____

_____

_____

_____

_____

_____

_____

_____

_____

APPLICATION 9–4: Proofreading Paragraphs

Rewrite the following paragraphs after proofreading carefully to clean up all errors. Explain why you made the changes you did and what the errors were.

> In steves beach photos the people appear to be in their late teens early twenties, and look a s they are having great time. They look as if they are partying and having fun It looks as they are on the beach because how the sand is every where. The Backround looks as, a fun, sandy place to dance;

Rewritten version:

_____

_____

_____

_____

_____

_____

_____

_____

_____

Revision explanation:

_____

_____

_____

_____

_____

_____

_____

_____

_____

Gourmet cooking is a serious enterprise: especially around the Holiday's. My family is small however; we have a large circle of friends, who all want to eat at our house whenever they can. So the phone rings constantly, whenever a holiday comes near—and people all want me to cook—candy, meat dishes, and vegetarian meals for them. They offer to pay, and I tell them to by the grocerys needed. Lists of grocerys can be two items or twenty items long with: wines, fruits, pasta, poultry; red meats, flavored oils; the list seems end less.

Rewritten version:

_____

_____

_____

_____

_____

_____

_____

_____

_____

_____

_____

_____

Revision explanation:

_____

_____

_____

_____

_____

_____

_____

_____

_____

As with all electrical fixture work: replacement and repair instruction's should be followed carefully use common sense. When preparing your work area: to avoid obvious dangers such as: water, sharp objects; inadequate tools; or rickety support structures. Take extra care when working. With electricity being sure, to ground your body and turn the electricity "off" on the Correct fuse before beginning, work; Keep all children and pet's away from the area—to avoid electrocution, or other injury.

Rewritten version:

_____

_____

_____

_____

_____

_____

_____

_____

_____

_____

_____

_____

_____

Revision explanation:

_____

_____

_____

_____

_____
_____
_____
_____
_____
_____

Claire and Nick are fascinated on costume design. Today they were working, on a costume project with their friends. It's a tough costume—a medieval knight's armor—and they have to cut and solder metal pieces at least I think thats what they do to each other. No room for buttons and bows: but lots of flames, shrieks, and intense concentration I guess to sew is'nt the only thing you do in costume design: their is allot of reserch to. Every one has to look up the history of armor to no what they're doing.

Rewritten version:

_____
_____
_____
_____
_____
_____
_____
_____
_____
_____
_____

_____

_____

Revision explanation:

_____

_____

_____

_____

_____

_____

_____

_____

_____

The swan glided acrost the pond and walked up to the picnic table. Where it bit Joseph right on the—well you now where. And anyway it, kept flapping it's wings but it didn't fly away instead: it just kept biting people and honking. It looked more graceful, wen it swam. How were the people going to go to the park again.

Rewritten version:

_____

_____

_____

_____

_____

_____

_____

_____

_____

Revision explanation:

_____

_____

_____

_____

_____

_____

_____

Twenty people surrounded me anxiously, peering over my shoulders to see what was in the cloth bag. Gingerly I pulled open the drawstring and the bag moved I almost dropped it. By this time my hands, were shaking? It's a good thing I'm a professional snake handler, because the rattlesnake could have bitten me or someone, else. It was a beautiful snake: covered in golden diamonds and a wide head and narrow snout. It was almost six-feet long, two; The snake slithered off into the saguaros, when I released it from the bag, and people jumped in all directions shrieking. They calmed down though when, they realized the reptile wasn't going to bite them it just wanted to get away from the crowd. Who wouldn't. We were glad to have gotten it off the highway and safely onto the desert.

Rewritten version:

_____

_____

_____

_____

_____

_____

_____

_____

_____

_____

_____

_____

_____

_____

_____

_____

Revision explanation:

_____

_____

_____

_____

_____

_____

_____

_____

_____

The following paragraphs contain no punctuation at all, which makes them more challenging to revise and proofread. However, follow the same instructions with them as you did with the above paragraphs.

Digital cameras well I guess they offer me more flexibility than film cameras but I also need a computer with a lot of hard drive space and I cant afford one right now so how am I going to do my photography should I keep using the film camera I still have lots of film but may be I should just use a digital camera borrow it from some one maybe jack will let me use his computer a easy computer to use for me any way

Rewritten version:

_____

_____

_____

_____

_____

_____

_____

_____

_____

Revision explanation:

_____

_____

_____

_____

_____

_____

_____

_____

_____

The annual bird count takes place in our city and in surrounding marshlands to give us an idea of what birds live where and on how urban development has impacted their breeding nesting and feeding patterns well start at six oclock in the morning to make sure to get all major birding areas volunteers have to provide their own lunches but bird list forms pencils measuring and banding equipment and netting are all provided by the participating organizations and vans will bring people in to the count areas

Rewritten version:

_____

_____

_____

_____

_____

_____

_____

_____

_____

_____

_____

_____

Revision explanation:

_____

_____

_____

_____

_____

_____

_____

_____

_____

I havent figured out my major yet because I have so many interests some are in mathematics and the sciences others are in the arts and humanities how can I combine philosophy and math what careers can I find that help me use all my interests what courses do I need to take and what about athletics and other outdoor activities is there a hiking club here what are the hiking areas in this location how about housing should I live on or off campus can I afford my own apartment I really want my own apartment and a place to park my car without having to pay for parking at home and at school

Rewritten version:

_____

_____

_____

_____

_____

_____

Revision explanation:

Now choose paragraphs of your own and do the above exercise with them. I've provided space below for you to revise three paragraphs; however, you may use notebook paper for this application if you prefer.

APPLICATION 9–5: Proofreading Your Own Paragraphs

Choose a paragraph that you have written and proofread it carefully. First, write the old version. Second, make notes and changes on it. Third, write out the new, proofread version. When you are finished, have someone else read the proofread draft and circle any errors or other problems you missed. Revise the paragraph again. Do this as many times as you need to, and whenever you have questions, *ask*!

Original paragraph:

_____

_____

_____

_____

_____

_____

_____

_____

_____

_____

_____

_____

_____

Rewritten version:

_____

_____

_____

_____

_____

_____

_____

_____

_____

_____

_____

_____

_____

_____

APPLICATION 9–6: Small-Group Proofreading

In a small group of three or four people, all of you proofread the same paragraph. Then discuss what each of you changed and why.

Endnote

1. *Games Magazine*, 1984.

CHAPTER 10

Format
Professional Presentation

Have compassion for yourself when you write. There is no
failure—just a big field to wander in.
—*Natalie Goldberg*

PART 1: WHAT'S THE POINT?

What is *professional presentation* and why should you care?
Professional presentation is how neat, clean, and audience-
appropriate your work looks at first glance. If it's a mess, you
will lose your readers' confidence. A mess suggests careless-
ness, lack of attention to detail, insecurity with the subject
matter, and a general lack of skill.

HOW YOUR PRESENTATION AFFECTS YOUR READERS

When carpenters frame houses, they must measure and square carefully and tightly attach all parts. If the framing looks like it will fall apart, then the carpenter is going to lose the confidence of clients—and therefore lose business.

When basketball coaches train athletes, they need to be detailed about strategies, make sure the players are working as a team, and keep morale high. Otherwise, their teams won't play well, the players will lose morale, and the coaches will lose their jobs.

When teachers do not know their material, students lose confidence in them.

When a dry cleaner returns your clothes stained or torn, you will not do any more business with him.

All of the above scenarios are examples of what can happen when attention is not paid to the details.

Consistency and Audience Expectations
Always give your audience what you say you will give them—this is being consistent.

FORMATTING BASICS

When formatting a paragraph, indent the first line three to five spaces (usually) and use 1″ margins (usually).

Margins   Generally, a 1-inch *margin* on all sides is used in formal writing. Unfortunately, the right and left margin settings in many word-processing programs are incorrectly set (default setting) at 1.25 inches. You should manually change the margin settings to 1 inch when you create a document (paragraph, essay, etc.).

For writing that is going to be bound, writers use a 1.5-inch margin setting for the left margin only (1 inch for the other three sides). This is because .5 inch is covered by the binding material (the cover). This is common for theses, dissertations, and book manuscripts.

Alignment   **Alignment** simply means how the words on a page line up. You can align phrases, sentences, paragraphs, bulleted items, lists in charts, and many other parts of texts. In order to align anything, you need to use some sort of formatting that keeps words in a straight line, such as tabs or tables.

Justification   **Justification** refers to the part of the page that the text is aligned with:

Left: The text is lined up at the left margin (many English texts).

Right: The text is lined up at the right margin.

Centered: The text is centered on the page.

Justified: The text lines up at both the left and right margins. This can cause spacing to be uneven, however, so be careful when you use it.

Most of your college writing will be aligned at the left margin.

Titles   In writing, titles should be highlighted in one of three ways:

Italics = <u>underline</u> (do one, not both): books, plays, TV shows (but not individual episodes), long poems

Quotation marks only: song titles; magazine, newspaper, and journal articles; most poems; short stories; book chapters; unpublished speeches; essays; individual TV show episodes.

Capitalization: Use all capital letters for a title only when you cannot format it with underlining or italics.

Paragraph Indentation   Generally indent the first line of a double-spaced paragraph five to seven spaces or .5 inch (although many people use one tab, too). Do not put any extra space between paragraphs (in other words, just continue double spacing).

For single-spaced paragraphs, you should add extra space (i.e., double space) between paragraphs. Single-spaced paragraphs do not have to be indented.

Always indent the first line of each paragraph when you double space and skip a line between paragraphs when you single space; otherwise, your readers will not always be able to tell when one paragraph ends and the next begins.

Headings and Subheadings   Headings and subheadings are like mini-titles that you use to name sections of a paragraph or essay. They help to organize your writing for yourself and your readers. They also help readers to quickly locate parts of your text. For instance, the italics that begin this section are a subheading. The bold phrases are headings. Headings divide large sections of text, and subheadings divide smaller sections within the larger sections. Headings and subheadings are more often used in essays; however, sometimes paragraphs are long enough to need them.

Headers and Footers   **Headers** and/or **footers** are used when you want the page number (and sometimes your last name or part of the title) to show up automatically, usually in the upper right corner (header) or centered at the bottom (footer).

Headers go in the margin at the top of the page. Footers go in the margin at the bottom of the page.

White (or Negative) Space   **White space** (sometimes called negative space) is simply the space that has nothing (no writing or images) in it; it allows readers to rest their eyes. It's a balance: too little white space can be exhausting; too much can make the content appear childish and undeveloped.

Twelve-Point Font Size   A 12-point font size is the best size for general content, though you might use different sizes for headings, etc. Smaller font sizes are difficult for some people to read. Larger font sizes tend to look childish or like the writer is trying to cover up a lack of content development.

COMMON DOCUMENTATION STYLES: MLA AND APA

MLA stands for Modern Language Association, and MLA style is simply one of many documentation styles—but also one of the most commonly used. A documentation style is a way of setting up an essay, quoting and paraphrasing outside sources, and creating a bibliography page (called "Works Cited" in the case of MLA style).

APA stands for American Psychological Association, and it is also a common documentation style—with a few differences from MLA style.

You will not be using documentation styles too much at this point; at least, you probably won't be citing outside sources yet. However, whether you write a paragraph or essay, you still set it up in a certain way, with certain margins, font sizes, and so forth. This section will give you a few tips on the basics of document formatting in MLA and APA styles.

MLA

- Set your margins at 1" on all sides (top, bottom, left, and right).

- Indent the first line of each paragraph five spaces (if using a typewriter) or .5" (if using a word processor/computer).

■ Use a very specific first-page setup. You don't need a title page; instead, put all necessary information on the first page, as in the box below:

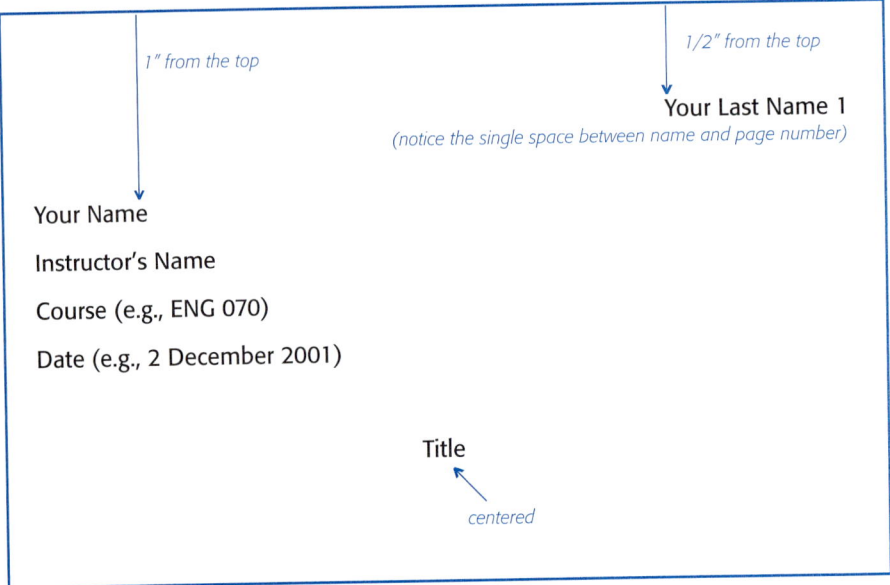

■ Center the title at the top of the page, 1″ from the top. Capitalize first and last words and all other words in the title except for indefinite and definite articles (a, an, the), prepositions (of, in, on, through, etc.), the "to" in verb infinitives (e.g., to run, to hover, to learn), and coordinating conjunctions (for, and, nor, but, or, yet, so). The only other time a word is capitalized is when it's the first word of a subtitle.

■ On all following pages, use an upper-right-margin header that includes your last name, one space, and the page number. (Do this also on your Works Cited page.)

APA

■ Set your margins at 1″ on all sides (top, bottom, left, and right).

■ Indent the first line of each paragraph five to seven spaces.

■ Use a separate title page with the following information centered on the page:

Title of your paper

Your first name, middle initial, and last name

The name of your school

- On the first page of the paper, center the title again at the top, 1" from the top of the page. In the title on this page and the title page, capitalize all the important words (nouns, verbs, adjectives, etc.) and all words with four or more letters. See the box below:

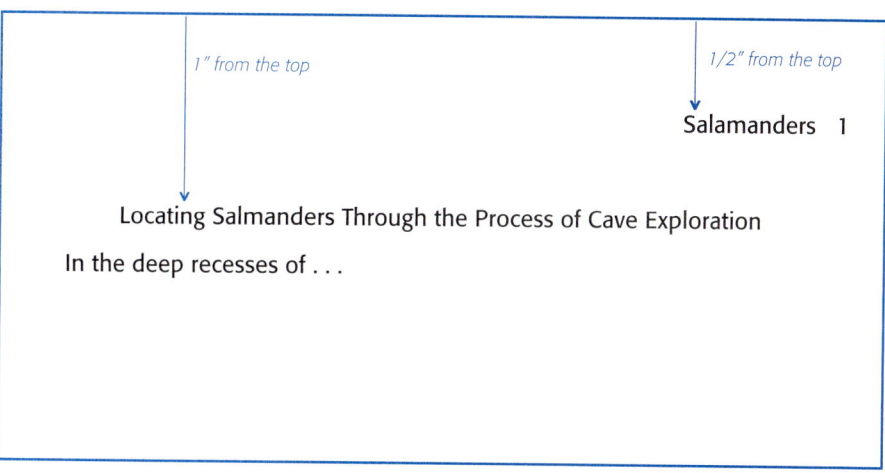

1" from the top   1/2" from the top

Salamanders   1

Locating Salmanders Through the Process of Cave Exploration

In the deep recesses of . . .

- In the upper right corner of each page (except for the title page), use a shortened version of the title and the page number. You can have a few spaces between them (unlike the one space of MLA style), but they should be on the same line. See the box above.

PART 2: APPLICATIONS

Formatting is a major part of professional presentaion, and the following activities will help you work individually and in groups with general, MLA, and APA formatting styles.

APPLICATION 10–1:   Designing a Paragraph Layout

Design a paragraph layout (including a title) for a variety of reading audiences. This means that you will use fonts, styles, white space, and headings differently depending on your imagined readers.

_____

_____

_____

_____

_____

_____

_____

_____

_____

_____

APPLICATION 10–2:   Small-Group Discussion of Formatting

In a small group, discuss and write down how the following paragraph should be reformatted according to the suggestions in this chapter:

"WORKING With electricity iN the House"
          As with all Electrical Fixture work, replacement and repair instructions should be followed carefully. Use common sense when preparing your work area to avoid obvious dangers such as water, sharp objects, inadequate tools, or rickety support structures. Take extra care when working with electricity, being sure to ground your body and turn the electricity off

at the correct fuse before beginning work. Keep all children and pets away from the area to avoid electrocution or other injury.

_____

APPLICATION 10–3: Documentation-Style Setup

Set up title/first pages in MLA and APA styles for the paragraph in Application 10–2.

_____

APPLICATION 10–4: Using Subheadings

Create a series of paragraphs that are linked together with subheadings. Think about logical places for the subheadings and relevant information that goes within the subheadings.

_____

_____

_____

_____

_____

_____

_____

_____

_____

_____

_____

_____

_____

_____

_____

_____

_____

_____

_____

_____

_____

_____

_____

_____

_____

_____

_____

_____

_____

APPLICATION 10–5: Text Justification

Write a paragraph explaining the problem with using evenly justified text (where both left and right margins are aligned):

_____

_____

_____

_____

_____

_____

_____

_____

_____

_____

Glossary

Most of these terms can be found in this book. However, some terms, though not included elsewhere in this text, are still concepts that you will encounter at some point in the classroom.

Alignment Alignment is when the beginnings of lines on a page line up evenly (or not). (p. 171)

Analogy Compares similarities between two unlike things or ideas in order to create a vivid description. (p. 91)

Analysis Explores how the various parts of a topic relate to each other; explains how and why supporting examples are significant. (pp. 15, 94)

APA The abbreviation for American Psychological Association, a documentation style used commonly in the social sciences (such as Family Studies). (p. 173)

Audience Your reader or readers. (pp. 5, 17, 27)

Audience awareness How conscious you are of the people you are writing to. The more aware you are of your readers—their expectations, likes and dislikes, backgrounds, ages, and reading situations—the more effectively you will reach those readers. (p. 6)

Brainstorming The invention that you do before composing your first draft. (pp. 36, 59, 70)

Clause Part of a sentence that has at least a subject and a verb. Clauses can be independent (can stand alone as sentences) or dependent (are only part of a complete thought and cannot stand alone as sentences). (p. 114)

Clustering A form of brainstorming in which you chart out a central idea or topic in a circle and then place related ideas, topics, and examples in smaller circles around the central one. Once that is done, you can draw lines connecting related items. (p. 61)

Coherence Clear and logical connections between ideas. (p. 22)

Colloquialism A word or phrase used in informal writing or conversation that is not part of Standard English. Colloquialisms should be avoided in many types of formal writing. (p. 90)

Compose To write or otherwise create a first draft of a text. (p. 16)

Conclusion/Concluding thought Brings a written passage to a smooth close. Any conclusion should be thoughtful, leaving the reader with an insight or question to ponder or a new perspective about the topic. In a paragraph a conclusion is often just one sentence long. (p. 15)

Connotation The emotional or otherwise personal associations you might have with a word based on your own experience. For instance, a particular brand of truck might have negative or positive connotations depending on whether it ran well for you or was always breaking down. (p. 71)

Content The substance of any text you write: all the details, idea development, examples, and analyses.

Content development How thorough and detailed the content of a text is. The more developed the content, the more effective the text. (pp. 8, 87)

Context What influences the way you write, what you write about, and how others interpret your writing. Context takes many forms: historical (time), geographical (place), linguistic (language), external social pressures, internal pressures, personal or professional environment, age, cultural background, spiritual beliefs, etc. (pp. 34, 56)

Credibility How believable, convincing, and professional your writing is to your readers. (pp. 32, 112)

Critique In terms of writing, to read a piece of writing carefully, taking notes, pointing out strengths, and making specific suggestions for improvement. (p. 102)

Definite article "The" in English. "The" designates a specific (definite) item, place, action, person, or idea. (pp. 2, 125)

Denotation The literal definition (specific meaning) of a word. (p. 71)

Dependent clause Part of a sentence that has a subject and a verb or verb phrase (predicate) but that does not form a complete thought. Therefore, it cannot stand alone as a sentence. (p. 114)

Diction Word choice.

Dictionary A book that lists words, their literal definitions (denotations), and their pronunciations. (pp. 26, 71, 124)

Draft A version of any text you are writing. Drafts can range all the way from first to final, with many drafts in between. (p. 16)

Drafting The composing process, where the writer is getting ideas on paper at any stage of a written work's development. (p. 60)

ESL The abbreviation for "English as a second language." (pp. 4, 5)

Examples Very specific stories, quotations, objects, or ideas that are used to support a claim that a writer makes. (pp. 15, 84, 103)

Focus The extent to which a writer stays true to his or her subject and does not get off track or try to write about too much or too little. (pp. 70, 82, 103)

Focused freewriting Still freewriting, but about a very specific topic. (pp. 63, 66)

Footer Information that is placed in the bottom margin of a page (such as the page number). (p. 173)

Form The type of document you write (e.g., letter, memo, essay). (p. 34)

Format The professional structure of a text: margins; pagination; font size and style; spacing; alignment; justification; use of titles, headings, and subheadings. (p. 36)

Freewrite A method of brainstorming in which you write for a specific length of time without stopping yourself for any reason. This form of writing allows you to get your ideas out without editing them too soon or shutting yourself down. (p. 62)

Grammar The theory of how words and phrases should be formed and put together in order to write as clearly as possible in any situation. (pp. 2, 52)

Header Information that is placed in the top margin of a page (such as your last name and the page number). (p. 173)

Homonyms Words that sound alike but are spelled differently and have different meanings. An example of a pair of homonyms is "sense" and "cents" (and some would include "since"). (p. 127)

Implication The suggested, indirect meaning of a word or phrase. Implication is often used to create an ironic, sarcastic, or suspenseful tone.

Indefinite article "A" or "an" in English. An indefinite article is used to designate a nonspecific (indefinite) item, place, action, person, or idea. "A" goes before a consonant sound, and "an" goes before a vowel sound. (pp. 2, 125)

Independent clause Part of a sentence that has a subject and a verb or verb phrase (predicate) and also forms a complete thought. It can stand alone as a sentence or be combined with another independent or a dependent clause. (p. 114)

Infer A verb meaning to draw a conclusion (receive an implication).

Invention The discovery work you do before composing a first draft. Invention can be a form of prewriting; however, it can also involve other activities, such as speaking into a tape recorder, drawing pictures of your ideas, discussing your ideas with another person, etc. (p. 59)

Journal (Noun) Any object onto or into which you can record your ideas in writing, by speaking, or by drawing. Although not used this way in the book, a journal is also a professional publication within a particular professional field or discipline. Articles in such a journal are written for fellow experts in the field. (Verb) The act of recording your ideas. (p. 41)

Justification Where alignment occurs—on the left or right margin (left justified or right justified), at both margins (justified), or in the center (centered). (p. 172)

Limited English proficiency (LEP) Having a knowledge of English but unable to read, write, and/or speak it easily. (p. 7)

Listing Writing a list of any words and ideas that come to mind about a topic. (p. 61)

Long vowel sound Vowels (a, e, i, o, u) have what are called long and short sounds, which depend on how the mouth shapes them. An example of a long vowel sound is the *i* in dining (as in eating). Notice, too, that there is only one *n* in "dining"; if there were two *n*'s, the *i* would be pronounced with a short sound: "dinning," as in "din," or loud noise. Here are the basic long vowel sounds: "ay" (as in "say"), "ee" (as in "sweet"), "eye" (as in "fine"), "oh" (as in "flow"), and "you" (as in "unicorn"). Vowel sounds affect both pronunciation and spelling. (p. 123)

Magazine A periodical (published periodically). Many magazines address special interest areas like fashion, gardening, and cars; however, they are intended to be read by the general public. (p. 41)

MLA The abbreviation for Modern Language Association, a documentation style used commonly in English and other liberal arts courses. (p. 173)

Mode of discourse A form of writing that uses language in a specific way and for a specific purpose: classification, description, narration, analysis, exemplification, comparison/contrast, cause/effect, process, definition, and argumentation/persuasion are all modes of discourse. (pp. 21, 193)

Organization The way in which a writer's ideas connect to one another, transition one to the next, and are prioritized. For instance, if its ideas are scattered, the text is poorly organized. (pp. 75, 81–82, 103)

Outline A method of setting out and organizing the topics in a piece of writing. Outlines help writers see whether their ideas flow smoothly and make sense. An outline generally uses Roman numerals, letters, and numbers to organize parts of a text from general to specific. (pp. 64, 75)

Paragraph A passage of writing that develops one topic and stays focused on that topic (though the topic itself can be discussed for more than one paragraph). Essays are composed of paragraphs. Most paragraphs have a topic sentence. (pp. 15, 34)

Peer evaluation The act of sharing your writing with one or more people, though usually no more than about three to five, so that they may give you their impressions of how close your writing is to fulfilling the assignment and offer specific suggestions for improvement. (p. 102)

Periodical Any text published in issues—daily, weekly, monthly, quarterly, etc. Magazines, professional journals, and newspapers are all periodicals. (p. 41)

Persuade The verb form of persuasion; it means to bring your readers around to your point of view by presenting clear, connected, well-supported ideas and arguments in your writing. (p. 33)

Persuasion What causes a reader to come around to your perspective or at least listen to you. The more persuasive you are, the more your writing will positively influence your readers. (p. 196)

Persuasive Describes writing that makes a strong enough impact on a person or people to make them listen and perhaps change their minds about a situation. (p. 6)

Phrasing How writers put words together, clearly or unclearly, to form thoughts. (p. 82)

Portfolio A compilation of various pieces of your writing—paragraphs, essays, poems, articles, or a combination. Portfolios are sometimes turned in to instructors for grades or used to show writing samples when applying for jobs. (p. 102)

Preposition A word that creates a relationship between parts of a sentence. It can be hard to define a preposition by itself; it is defined by the context in which it is used. Some prepositions are "in," "of," "on," "over," "at," "to," "beyond," and "through."(p. 124)

Prewriting The discovery writing you do before first composing a draft. This can take many forms: listing, freewriting, clustering, outlining, etc. (p. 59)

Pronunciation The way words and parts of words (vowels, consonants, syllables) sound in any particular language. (p. 123)

Proofread To identify and clean up sentence-level errors: typos; spelling, punctuation, and format errors; and any missed grammatical errors. You should *always* proofread after you have finished revision, and before submitting your writing to another reader. Proofreading may also be done during the composing and revising processes. (pp. 16, 60)

Prose A term to describe writing that is not poetry (e.g., sentences, paragraphs, essays). (p. 56)

Punctuation The small symbols that help writers form effective sentences and create clear meanings. Examples of punctuation marks are periods, semicolons, and apostrophes. (pp. 52, 82, 112)

Purpose The underlying reason for any piece of writing. Generally, an effective written work makes its purpose clear in the introduction. (p. 33)

Résumé A formal listing of your work, educational, and other experiences as they relate to a job you are applying for. (pp. 22, 33)

Revise To work on the organization, content development, style, and major grammatical issues of a piece of writing. Revision often is done more than once. (pp. 16, 20)

Revision Extensive work on a piece of writing that improves its organization, content development, style, and grammar. (pp. 16, 60, 81, 102)

Short vowel sound Vowels (a, e, i, o, u) have what are called long and short sounds, which depend on how the mouth shapes them. An example of a short vowel sound is the *e* in "letter." It's pronounced like "eh." If you pronounced the *e* (or *e*'s) in "sweet," then you'd be producing a long vowel sound. Here are the basic short vowel sounds: "aaa" (as in "as"), "eh" (as in "yet"), "ih" (as in "is"), "ah" (as in "on"), and "uh" (as in "unload"). Vowel sounds affect both pronunciation and spelling. (p. 123)

Standard English Written and spoken English used in formal situations and according to very specific rules of grammar and style. Generally used in college writing. (p. 1)

Style The way vocabulary is used, words are phrased, and sentences are constructed. Depending on how effectively the writer does these things, the text can range from clear and smoothly flowing to impossible to understand. (pp. 5, 52, 81, 82–83)

Support The examples, analysis, and other elements you use to develop and back up your topic sentence. (p. 32)

Syntax How words are put together and sentences are phrased.

Thesaurus A book that lists words and other words that have similar meanings. When using a thesaurus, however, it is important to make sure the words can actually be substituted for one another; just because they may have similar meanings does not mean that they have the exact same meaning. (p. 71)

Tone The attitude in a piece of writing. How do you sound on paper? Cold? Warm? Angry? Inviting? Accessible? Exclusive? Pompous? That is the tone. (pp. 5, 32, 36, 56)

Topic An idea or subject that is explored in a paragraph or essay. (p. 15)

Topic sentence Gives the central idea/topic of a paragraph. The topic sentence usually is the first sentence of the paragraph. (pp. 15, 72–73, 82, 103)

Transition A word or phrase that lets your readers know you are moving on to a new paragraph (and most likely a new topic). (pp. 15, 73–74)

Transitional words Words that help writers move from one idea to the next and that signal readers a change in ideas is coming (e.g., "therefore," "however," "and," "but," "or"). (pp. 73, 116)

Typographical error (typo) A mistake such as an omitted letter or an extra space that needs to be fixed during proofreading. (p. 121)

Unity In writing, how clearly and smoothly ideas are connected to one another. (pp. 21, 70–74)

Vocabulary The words you use—and how effectively or ineffectively you use them. (pp. 36, 52, 82)

White space Empty space in a text—margins, breaks between paragraphs, space around images. (p. 173)

Wordiness Using too many words in various written phrases, such as using six words where two or three will do. Here is an example of wordiness: "The plane that was flying me home went over some tall mountains." This sentence can be rewritten as, "The plane I was on flew over a mountain range," or even, "My plane flew over a mountain range." (p. 82)

Workshop A form of peer evaluation in which a group of writers submit their writing to each other in order to brainstorm and discover other ideas for revising their writing. It can be done in person or online. (p. 102)

Business and Technical Writing

In your careers, you will write many documents, and certain guidelines apply to their correct use.

CLEAR STYLE

Clear style means that the vocabulary that writers use is understandable and readable by several audiences, probably with educational backgrounds ranging from high school to graduate school (see "middle style," page 56). Not too many technical terms (jargon) are used in plain-style documents because these documents are not intended only for experts. Sentences in plain style are not wordy; they flow smoothly and get their points across quickly (without elaborate phrasing or vocabulary). Plain style still sounds intelligent; however, it is accessible to a wide variety of educated readers.

WORDS COMMONLY CONFUSED

See pages 127–128 for a list of commonly confused words.

When you write a memo or letter for work, it is essential that you proofread it before sending it out. One area to focus on when proofreading is words that are commonly confused with one another. For example, do you mean "accept" or "except"? Are you writing "form" or "from"? Is a procedure "allowed" or "aloud"? Is it "right" or "write"?

As you can see, it is easy to use "the wrong word spelled right," and you can quickly lose professional credibility with your readers if you are not careful to clean up errors.

WORD CHOICE AND TONE

Another area that requires close attention is the tone or attitude you create in writing. The words you use set the tone, making it range from casual to formal, emotional to emotionless. In business and technical writing, writers generally do *not* use clichés or slang, no matter how casual they intend to be. You want your letters, memos, and other work documents to sound professional even when relaxed. On the other hand, using vocabulary that is full of multisyllabic words and jargon can sound arrogant and pompous, alienating the very people you want to connect with.

You may find yourself writing to employees, supervisors, company presidents, bankers, customers, and many other individuals. Think carefully about who your audience is for any particular document—audiences change—and what that audience expects and needs to know. In any writing situation, the clearer you are about whom you're writing to, the more appropriate your tone will be.

LETTERS AND MEMOS

Letters and memos are two of the most commonly written professional documents. Each document has a specific format that you need to follow.

Letters

Letters may be written in block style or modified block style. Paragraphs may be either indented or not. *Block style* means that the closing salutation is aligned with the left margin. *Modified block style* means that the closing salutation is aligned with the heading at the top of the page.

Letters begin with a heading, either centered at the top of the page or aligned at the left margin. This contains the sender's (*not* the recipient's) name and complete address. You may include e-mail addresses and phone/fax numbers in the heading or in the concluding paragraph.

Directly below the head, type the date. You may use the American style, which places the month first (May 16, 2002) or the international style, which places the day first and does not use a comma (16 May 2002).

If you want to use a subject or reference line, skip *one* line after the heading and type "Subject:" followed by a phrase that sums up the letter's purpose.

Skip *one* line and type the recipient's name, professional title (if you know it), and address just as you will type them on the mailing envelope.

Skip *one* line and type the greeting (opening salutation) aligned with the left margin. Usually, the greeting is simply comprised of "Dear," the person's formal name and title, and a *colon*. However, in an informal situation with someone whose first name you use, you may type "Dear," the person's first name, and a *comma*.

Skip *one* line and begin the introductory paragraph of the letter. After this paragraph skip *one* line and begin the first body paragraph of the letter. Skip *one* line between each paragraph. End the letter with a concluding paragraph. (Note: In letters, opening or concluding paragraphs are sometimes one or two lines.)

Skip *one* line after the concluding paragraph and type the closing salutation, which is usually "Sincerely." When using block style, align the closing salutation with the left margin. In modified block style, align it with the header.

Skip *four* lines and type your name then your title below it, both aligned with "Sincerely." The four lines of space allow room for your signature.

If you have enclosed any other documents with the letter, you need to indicate this, too. Skip *one* line after your name and type "Enclosure:" followed by *one* space and a description of the enclosed document(s). Capitalize the first word of the document:

Enclosure: Résumé

If you are sending copies of the letter to someone else, skip *one* line after your name and type "cc:" followed by *one* space, then followed by an aligned list of the names and titles:

cc: Martin Begay, Associate Director
     Loretta Wilton, Associate Director

If you are doing both, do not separate them; just type "Enclosure" first:

Enclosure: Résumé
cc: Martin Begay, Associate Director
     Loretta Wilton, Associate Director

See the following models of block and modified block styles:

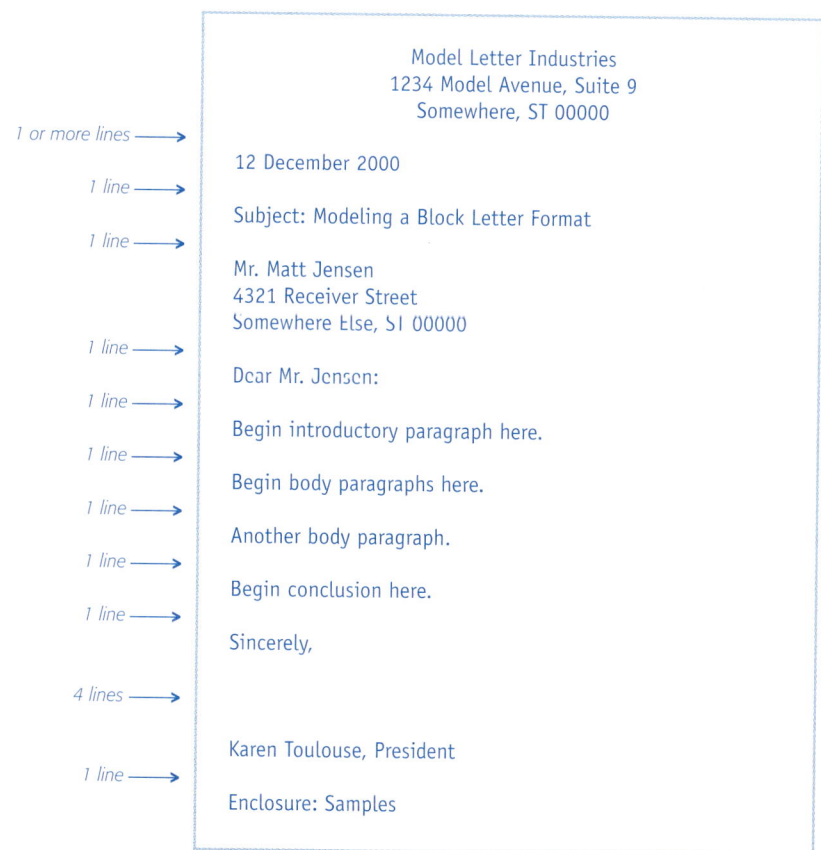

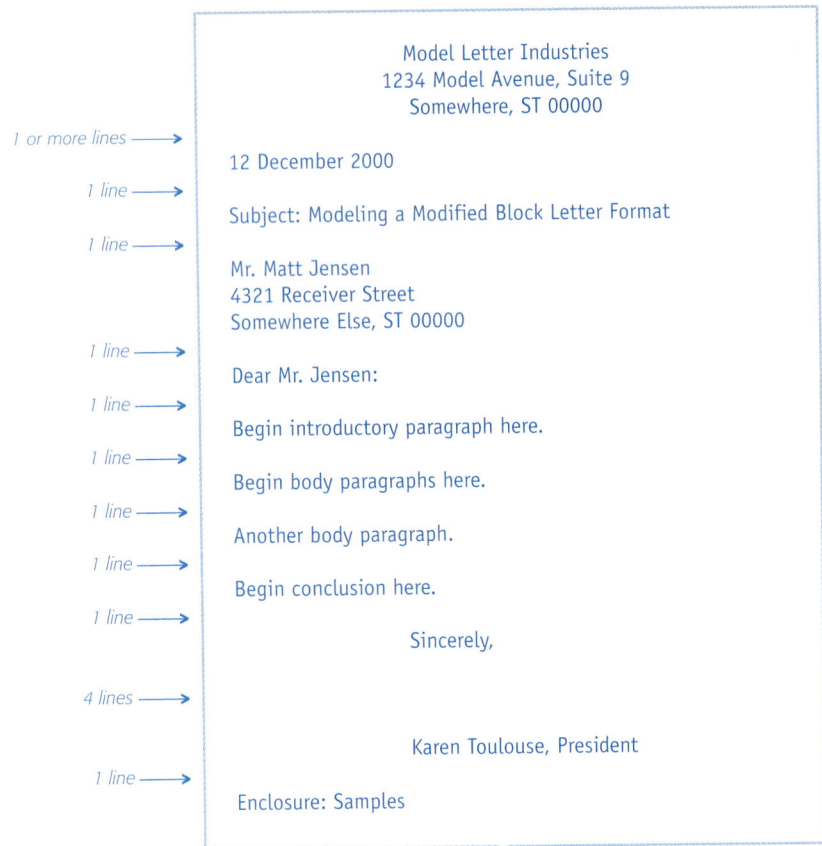

Model Letter Industries
1234 Model Avenue, Suite 9
Somewhere, ST 00000

1 or more lines ———▶

12 December 2000

1 line ———▶

Subject: Modeling a Modified Block Letter Format

1 line ———▶

Mr. Matt Jensen
4321 Receiver Street
Somewhere Else, ST 00000

1 line ———▶

Dear Mr. Jensen:

1 line ———▶

Begin introductory paragraph here.

1 line ———▶

Begin body paragraphs here.

1 line ———▶

Another body paragraph.

1 line ———▶

Begin conclusion here.

1 line ———▶

Sincerely,

4 lines ———▶

Karen Toulouse, President

1 line ———▶

Enclosure: Samples

Memos

Memos are also used for many purposes: to send private information, to report an incident, to sum up a meeting, etc. Just as letters do, memos follow a basic format.

At the top, either centered or aligned with the left margin, you may type the word "Memo" or "Memorandum" (depending on how formal you want to be). Don't include the quotation marks. On some business stationery, the memo heading is already provided; do not retype it if this is the case.

Skip *four* to *five* lines and type "Date:" "To:" "Cc:" "From:" and "Subject:" (or "RE:"), skipping *one* line between each of these headings. Don't include the quotation marks.

Skip *one* line and begin the opening paragraph. *Single space* paragraphs, skipping *one* line between each. You may indent the first line of each paragraph or not, as you prefer, but be consistent. As with letters, memos should have introductions, bodies, and conclusions; be clearly written; and be carefully proofread.

Write your initials after your name in the "From:" line to indicate that you have read and approved this memo before sending it out. Another option is to sign the memo at the bottom; however, this method is less common.

Here is an example of a basic memo setup:

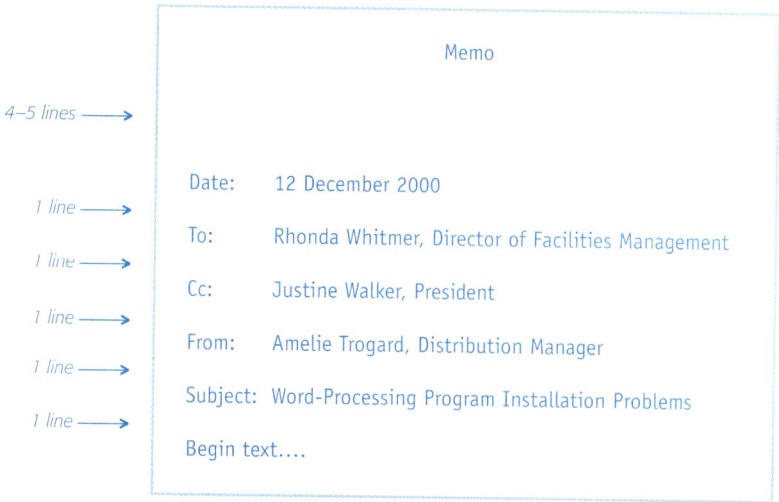

Memo

4–5 lines ⟶

Date: 12 December 2000

1 line ⟶

To: Rhonda Whitmer, Director of Facilities Management

1 line ⟶

Cc: Justine Walker, President

1 line ⟶

From: Amelie Trogard, Distribution Manager

1 line ⟶

Subject: Word-Processing Program Installation Problems

1 line ⟶

Begin text....

A Note about E-Mail

E-mail follows the same basic format as memos do. One very important reminder, however, is to proofread your e-mail messages extremely carefully before pressing the "send" button. Sometimes, too, you might want to wait before sending a message, particularly if it is about a sensitive or heated situation. Once you press "send," you can't get your message back, so don't set yourself up to get fired or otherwise put yourself at risk.

Modes of Discourse/ Rhetorical Modes

The phrases "modes of discourse" and "rhetorical modes" simply refer to the methods of exploring and writing about a topic. Well-written texts combine a variety of modes. Below, however, I will discuss nine of these methods separately so that you have a clear idea of how each is used.

Let's look at this paragraph from Christina Payson (chapter 2) again:

> At the beginning of every school year, I would get a new pair of shoes. Third grade came along, and with it the white Reebok high-tops with the two Velcro straps at the top of the shoe. These lasted much longer than Keds, and not only were girls wearing them, so were mothers. I thought I was so cool with my fluorescent socks and white tennis shoes. In fourth grade I got the new "double tongues" Reeboks. They were lavender and white. Nothing special, except they had an extra tongue that covered the laces when they were tied. New Kids on the Block and slap bracelets were the current trends, and I had my fill of both. My questions were more complex. Why do we really need to know how to write in cursive? And we're in fourth grade now (out of the primary grades), so why does the teacher still feel the need to have the alphabet on the top of the chalkboard? I never would have guessed that the alphabet would still be there in high school. I think I genuinely cared about school because the grades were "real" letter grades, not E+ or S–, and we got to carry a Trapper Keeper binder instead of the school-provided folders. I didn't watch cartoons anymore. I was at a dance or soccer or softball or swim team. That was the period where anything to tire us out would come in handy, to my mom.

This passage from Christina's essay uses a variety of rhetorical modes: classification, description, narration, analysis, and exemplification.

CLASSIFICATION

Classification creates categories to group together characteristics of a topic. In her essay (see pages 17–18 to look at more passages from the essay), Christina divides parts of her childhood by the shoes she wears at different stages of her childhood. She is arguing that "shoes are the strong memory that ties to my personality at a specific time. Through shoes I can easily relate to where and who I was in my life." The first section of the essay is organized under "Keds"; the next under "Reeboks" (which is repeated above); and so forth. This is an example of classification used in a personal essay. You might have used classification in science papers at some point, organizing an organism by phylum, genus, and species, for example.

DESCRIPTION

Christina uses a great deal of description, too. In the above Reebok paragraph, she describes the shoes she wore in fourth grade as "high-tops with the two Velcro straps," having "double tongues," colored "lavender and white," and looking "so cool" with her "fluorescent socks." All of these details are examples of description; Christina uses them to help her readers more easily picture her shoes in their minds.

The more concrete and specific words and phrases are, the more effective description is. For example, in *The Moon by Whale Light*, author and naturalist Diane Ackerman describes a cup of coffee as being "strong enough to trot a mouse across."[1] What an image! It will stay in many readers' minds for a long time simply because it is so strong and unusual. That is an excellent example of description.

NARRATION

Narration explores a topic either by telling a story about it or presenting it as a story. Christina uses narration in her paragraph when she writes about the "more complex" questions she asks in fourth grade. Her list of questions is gently ironic and humorous—as is the entire essay—developing the general tone and atmosphere first set up in the introductory narrative:

> When my mom is talking to people, she notices what color their clothes are. When my best friend is talking to people, she observes what type of jewelry they are wearing. When I am talking to people, I always seem to know what shoes they have on.

Narration helps readers imagine how characters are interacting with each other and how events are taking place. Along with description it creates atmosphere and tone.

ANALYSIS

The mode of analysis explores the various parts of a topic to determine how they relate to one another and how they might form a larger meaning.

College writing will ask you to use analysis a lot, and Christina's essay incorporates some analysis in her use of shoes to represent her growing maturity. The shoes allow her to discuss what she is like at each age, to reveal ways in which she thinks, and generally to represent the significance of each time period in her life. Analysis often involves asking "how" and "why." By showing her readers *how* shoes represent life stages, Christina shows her readers *why* they are so significant to her.

EXEMPLIFICATION

Exemplification develops a topic by offering examples and expanding on them. Not only are styles of shoes representative of Christina's childhood and young adulthood, they offer functional examples by which she can organize her entire essay. The topic is about how shoes represent significant stages of her life and also help her distinguish between them. The examples used to organize this topic are varieties of shoes.

COMPARISON/CONTRAST

You are probably already familiar with comparison/contrast, which explores similarities and differences between either parts of a topic or various topics. An example of comparison/contrast would be comparing a novel to the film version of the same novel. For example, *Frankenstein, or the Modern Prometheus* was written in 1816 by Mary Shelley, and the film *Mary Shelley's Frankenstein* was produced in 1994, almost 200 years later. If you were writing several comparison/contrast paragraphs about them, you might explore how the film was loyal to the novel and how it was different from the novel. You might also look at an earlier film version of *Frankenstein*, and compare/contrast it with both the novel and the other film. The purpose of comparison/contrast is not just to show differences and similarities but also to show what makes them important and meaningful.

CAUSE/EFFECT

This method of exploring a topic involves discussing what influences (causes) what, how these influences occur, and what the results (effects) are. For instance, a cause/effect paragraph about Mary Shelley and *Frankenstein, or the Modern Prometheus* might examine how her lifestyle in 1816 influenced the way she wrote the novel. Or, if you wanted to focus only on the novel itself, you could explore how Victor Frankenstein's obsession contributed to the "Monster's" despair and violent behavior.

PROCESS

If you are writing a process document, you are actually describing the steps by which something is done (its process). An example of this might be a retail store manager writing out the steps involved in opening and closing the cash register in a memo to his or her staff.

DEFINITION

In a document that uses definition (also called *extended definition*), the writer is literally defining a term—what it means and where and how it is used. This is common in technical writing, where writers frequently have to use technical terms with readers who do not necessarily understand them. For instance, writers of computer user manuals often use definition for terms like "modem," "RAM" (vs. "ROM"), and "processor," to name only four of thousands. If the writers did not define these terms and show how they are used, new computer users (and yes, there are some) would become confused and frustrated because they would have no idea what the writers were talking about.

ARGUMENTATION/PERSUASION

Quite often in college, you will be asked to take a particular stand or position on an issue and support it with relevant examples, thoughtful analysis, and thorough research. This process is referred to as "argumentation" or "persuasion." The purpose of argumentation/persuasion is to try to convince your readers to agree with your position; however, you cannot do this carelessly. You must present your claims and support them thoughtfully, reasonably, and with conviction. In addition, you must decide whether it is best to appeal to your readers' senses of logic (logos), ethics and credibility (ethos), or emotions (pathos). For most of your college writing, you will rely primarily on logic (i.e., careful research and thoughtful discussion) to persuade your readers. One important note is that, in this context, "argument" does NOT refer to starting or participating in a fight wits your readers.

The important point to remember about using modes of discourse is that it is natural to combine them in your writing. You might have been taught to write separately in each mode when you were first introduced to them, but this was only to familiarize you with the purpose of each method. It is not how most writing is created. As you become more familiar with the various modes, you will be able to choose how and when to use them in different writing situations.

Endnote

1. Diane Ackerman, *The Moon by Whale Light and Other Adventures among Bats, Penguins, Crocodilians, and Whales* (New York: Random House, 1991), 129.

More Resources about Writing

Aardvark's English Forum and EFL Resources. 16 August 2001 **http://www.english-forum.com/**.

Barrington, Judith. *Writing the Memoir: From Truth to Art.* Portland, Oreg.: Eighth Mountain Press, 1997.

Brande, Dorothea. *Becoming a Writer.* Reprinted 1981. Los Angeles: Jeremy P. Tarcher, Inc., 1934.

Cameron, Julia. *The Artist's Way: A Spiritual Path to Higher Creativity.* Los Angeles, Jeremy P. Tarcher, Inc., 1992.

Freelance Writers: Style Guides. 24 February 2002 **http://techwriting.about.com/cs/styleguides/**.

Goldberg, Natalie. *Living Color: A Writer Paints Her World.* New York: Bantam, 1997.

———. *Wild Mind: Living the Writer's Life.* New York: Bantam, 1990.

———. *Writing Down the Bones: Freeing the Writer Within.* Boston: Shambhala Publications, Inc., 1986.

Keen, Sam, and Anne Valley-Fox. *Your Mythic Journey: Finding Meaning in Your Life through Writing and Storytelling.* Los Angeles: Jeremy P. Tarcher, Inc., 1989.

Lamott, Anne. *Bird by Bird: Some Instructions on Writing and Life.* New York: Anchor-Doubleday, 1994.

Nelson, G. Lynn. *Writing and Being: Taking Back Our Lives through the Power of Language.* San Diego: LuraMedia, 1994.

Reeves, Judy. *A Writer's Book of Days: A Spirited Companion and Lively Muse for the Writing Life.* Novato, Calif.: New World Library, 1999.

Sperling, Dave, and Dennis Oliver. *ESL Idiom Page.* 16 August 2001 **http://www.pacificnet.net/~sperling/idioms.cgi**.

VLC Hong Kong Virtual Language Center 2001. 16 August 2001 **http://vlc.polyu.edu.hk/**.

Williams, Joseph M. *Style: Ten Lessons in Clarity and Grace.* 6th ed. New York: Longman, 2000.

Zinsser, William, ed. *Inventing the Truth: The Art and Craft of Memoir.* Boston: Houghton Mifflin Company, 1987.

Index

"A," 126
Abbreviations, 113
Ackerman, Diane, 194
ADD. *See* Attention-deficit disorder
Addresses, 115
Adjectives, singular and plural forms of, 122–123
Advertisement(s)
    analyzing, 47–48
    focused freewriting about, 66–67
    freewriting about, 66
    identifying and analyzing audiences for, 41–42
Age, of audience, 31
Alignment, 171
American Indians, 6
American Psychological Association (APA), 173, 174–175
American style date, 188
"An," 126
Analogy, 91, 92–94
Analysis, 16, 194–195
Anzaldúa, Gloria, 20–21
APA. *See* American Psychological Association
Apostrophe, 117–118, 137–139
Apprenticeship, 7
Argumentation, 196
Argument paper, 33
Atlantic Monthly, 2
Attention-deficit disorder (ADD), 4
Audience, 30, 31–32
    age of, 31
    background of, 31
    and content development, 87–89
    describing yourself as, 43–46
    draft written for, 17
    expectations of, 31–32
    identifying
        for advertisements, 41–42
        for coupons, 42
        through tone and vocabulary, 41
    paragraphs for different, 38–41
    professional presentation and, 171
    in storytelling, 5
Audience awareness, 6

Background noise, 60
Blocks, 61
Block style, 188, 189
Brainstorming, 36, 59
    during composing process, 65
    definition of, 60
    kinesthetic (movement), 61
    oral, 60
    visual, 60–61
    writing-based, 61–65
Business writing, 187–191

Capitalization, of titles, 172
Castilian Spanish, 2
Casual letter, 33
Cause/effect, 195
"cc:", 189
Ciliotta, Claire, 20, 24
Circular model of writing, 16
Classification, 193–194
Classroom, sharing work in, 102
Clauses, 114
Clear style, 187
Closing salutation, 188
Cluster, 61–62
    creating, 67–68
    focused, 68
Coherence, 22
Colloquialism, 90
Colon, 117, 135–137, 188
Colored blocks, 61
Comma, 114–115, 129–132, 188
Common sense, 20
Community gatherings, 6
Comparison/contrast, 195
Compound subjects, 123
Computer spell-check programs, 4, 128
Concluding thought, 16
Conjunctions, 114
Connotation, 71
Consonants, 123, 127
Content development, 87–89
Context, 30, 34–37
    definition of, 30
    and style, 56
Cosmopolitan, 33

Coupons, identifying and analyzing audiences for, 42
Credibility, 32–33, 112
Critiques, 102
Cultural background, of audience, 31

Dash, 120–121, 147–148
Dates, 115
    American style, 188
    international style, 188
Definite articles, 2, 125–127
Definition, 197
Denotation, 71
Dependent clause, 114
Description, 194
Dictionary, 26, 71, 124
Discussion
    facilitated, 109
    of formatting, 176–177
    open, 108–109
Documentation-style setup, 177
Drafts, 16
Drawing, 60
Dyslexia, 26

Either/or constructions, 123
Electronic test bank, xix
E-mail, 191
"Enclosure," 188–189
English-as-second-language (ESL) learners, language challenges for, 3–4
Enumeration, 21
Examples, 15, 84, 95, 195
Exclamation mark, 121
Expectations, of audience, 31–32
Expressions, idiomatic, 124
Extended definition, 197

Facilitated discussion, 109
Fear, 7
Filler words, 89
Florida State Exit Exam, xxi
Focus
    identifying from cluster, 68
    topic sentence and, 72–73, 82
Focused cluster, 68
Focused freewriting, 63–64
    about advertisement, 66–67
Font size, 173
Footers, 173
"For example," 74
Formal style, 56
Format, 170–179
Form of writing, 34
Freewriting, 62–63
    about advertisement, 66
    focused, 63–64
        about advertisement, 66–67
Full stop. See Period
"Furthermore," 73–74

Grammar, knowledge of, reading expanding, 52
Group-workshopping handout, 106–107
Group-workshopping styles/activities, 108–109

Handout
    group-workshopping, 106–107
    one-on-one peer evaluation, 107–108
Headers, 173
    APA style, 175
    MLA style, 174
Headings, 172–173
Henry, D. J., xxi
Homonyms, 4, 127–128, 187
How, asking, 12–14, 87
"However," 74
"How to Tame a Wild Tongue" (Anzaldúa), 20–21
Hymns, 5–6
Hyphen, 119–120, 149–150

Idea development, 90–91
Idea repetition, 90–91
Idioms, 124
Indefinite articles, 2, 125–127
Indentation of paragraphs, 172
    APA style, 174
    MLA style, 173
Independent clause, 114, 116
Instructor's manual, xvii
Internal concerns, 36–37
International style date, 188
Internet, workshops on, 102, 109
Invention, 59–69
    during composing process, 65
    learning styles and, 60–65
"In which," 83
Is It Dark? Is It Light? (Lankford), 51
Italics for titles, 172

Journal, 41
Justification, 172, 179

Kinesthetic (movement) brainstorming, 61

Language
    challenges in, 2–4
    of writing, 36
Lankford, Mary D., 51
Learning disability (LD), 4, 26
Learning styles, and invention, 60–65
Lectures, 6
Letters
    business, 188–189
    casual, 33
Limited English proficiency (LEP) learners, 7
Linear model of writing, 16
Listing, 61
Literacy, oral

definition of, 5
types of, 5–6
Livingston, Carole, 20, 24
Longman Electronic Newsletter, xix
Longman English Pages Web Site, xix
Longman Writer's Warehouse (website), xviii
Long sounds, 123

Magazine, 41
Magazine cover, analyzing, 48–49
"Many," 122
Margins, 171
  APA style, 174
  MLA style, 173
Maxim, 33
Meaning, 70–80
Memos, 190–191
Merriam Webster's Collegiate Dictionary,
  xvii–xviii
Middle style, 56
Modern Language Association (MLA),
  173–174
Modes of discourse, 193–196
"A Modest Proposal" (Swift), 34–36
Modified block style, 188, 190
The Moon by Whale Light (Ackerman), 194
Movement (kinesthetic) brainstorming, 61
"Much," 122

Narration, 194
National Geographic, 33
Negative space. *See* White space
"Neither...nor," 122
*The New American Webster Handy College
  Dictionary,* xvii
Newsweek, xviii
New Yorker, 2
New York Times, 2
Non-unified paragraph, 21–22, 72
Note cards, 61
Nouns, singular and plural forms of, 122

Omissions, 121
One-on-one peer evaluation, 103–104, 110
One-on-one peer evaluation handout,
  107–108
Open discussion, 108–109
Opening salutation, 188
Oral brainstorming, 60
Oral literacy
  definition of, 5
  types of, 5–6
Organization, 75, 82
Outlining, 64–65, 69, 75

Paragraph length
  myths and truths about, 19–21
  vs. thoroughness, 89
Paragraphs, 15–29, 34
  analyzing, 26–28

definition of, 15
designing layout of, 176
for different audiences, 38–41
with examples, 15, 84, 95
indentation of, 172
  APA style, 174
  MLA style, 173
ingredients of, 15–16
myths and truths about, 17–23
non-unified, 21–22, 72
proofreading exercises, 155–167
revising, 83–87
rewriting, 46–47
Parentheses, 119, 144–147
Payson, Christina, 17–19
Peer evaluation, one-on-one, 103–104, 110
Peer evaluation handout, 107–108
Penguin paperbacks, xviii
Period, 113–114
Periodicals, 41
Persuasion, 196
Persuasive paper, 33
Persuasive speeches, 6
Phrasing, 82
Place, of writing, 36
Plain style, 56
Plural forms
  of adjectives, 122–123
  of nouns, 122
  vs. possessive forms, 117–118
  of verbs, 121–122
Portfolios, 102, 105
Possessive forms, *vs.* plural forms, 117–118
Powwow, 6
Prefix, 120
Prepositions, 123, 124–125
Prewriting. *See* Brainstorming
Private-to-public model of writing, 16–17
Process document, 196
Professional presentation, of writing,
  170–179
Pronunciation, 4, 123–124
Proofreading, 4, 111–169
  definition of, 111
  e-mails, 191
  small-group, 169
Punctuation, 52, 82, 112–121
Purpose, of writing, 33, 47

Question mark, 118, 139–142
Questions, of peer evaluators, 103–104
Quotation marks, 118–119, 142–144, 172

Reading
  roundtable, 108
  and writing, 50–58
Reading aloud, 60, 102
Recipe, 33
Recording ideas, 60
Religious ceremonies, 5–6

Résumé, 33
Revision, 20, 81, 83–87
Rhetorical modes, 193–196
Roundtable reading, 108

Salutation
    closing, 188
    opening, 188
SE. *See* Standard English
Semicolon, 115–117, 132–135
Sentence, topic, 15, 72–73, 76–77, 82
Sentence fragment, 84
Sentence-level error, 84–85
Sermons, 5–6
Short sounds, 123
"Sincerely," 188
Singular forms, 121–123
Small-group formatting discussion, 176–177
Small-group meetings, 103
Small-group proofreading, 169
Smithsonian, 33
"Sometimes," 74
Speeches, 6
Spell-check programs, 4, 128
Spelling, 127–128
Standard English (SE), 2
Stanzas, 34
Storytelling, 5
Style, 82–83
    block, 188, 189
    clear, 187
    context and, 56
    formal, 56
    knowledge of, reading expanding, 52
    middle, 56
    modified block, 188, 190
    plain, 56
    of sermons and hymns, 5–6
Subconscious, 62
Subheadings, 172–173, 178–179
Subject-verb agreement, 123
Support, 32
Swift, Jonathan, 34–36

Taping ideas, 60
Technical writing, 187–191
Test bank, xvii, xix
"The," 125–126
Thesaurus, 71
Thinking Through the Test (Henry), xxii
Thoroughness, *vs.* paragraph length, 89

Time, of writing, 34–35
Title page
    APA style, 174
    MLA style, 174
Titles, 172
Tone, 32–33
    in business and technical writing, 187–188
    identifying audience through, 41
    of sermons and hymns, 5–6
Topic sentence, 15, 72–73, 76–77, 82
"To which," 83
Town council meetings, 6
Transition, 16, 22–23, 73–74
Transitional words, 73–74, 116
Twelve-point font size, 173
Typos, 121

Underlining titles, 172
Unity, 71–74
    definition of, 21
    lack of, 21–22, 72

Verbs, singular and plural forms of,
    121–122
Visual brainstorming, 60–61
Vocabulary, 82
    in clear style, 187
    identifying audience through, 41
    reading expanding, 52
Vowels, 123

"Walking in My Shoes" (Payson), 17–19
Wall Street Journal, 2
"Which," 83
White space, 17, 173
Why, asking, 12–14, 87
Why Am I Going to the Hospital? (Ciliotta and
    Livingston), 20, 24
Wordiness, 82
Words, 71
    in business and technical writing,
        187–188
    filler, 89
    transitional, 73–74, 116
Workshops, 102–103
    online, 102, 109
Writer's ToolKit Plus (CD-ROM), xviii
Writing backgrounds, exploring, 8–11
Writing-based brainstorming, 61–65
Writing process, 16–17
    brainstorming during, 65